4.50

Upholstery

A Step – by – Step Guide

Jeanne Argent

HAMLYN

London · New York · Sydney · Toronto

Published by the Hamlyn Publishing Group Ltd.
London · New York · Sydney · Toronto
Astronaut House, Feltham, Middlesex, England
© Copyright The Hamlyn Publishing Group Limited 1974

ISBN 0 600 38119 6

Printed in England by Chapel River Press (IPC Printers), Andover, Hampshire

Contents

Introduction

You may be interested in doing your own upholstery simply because your dining chairs are looking rather the worse for wear and it would be rather expensive to get them professionally repaired. On the other hand you may be the sort of person who is always looking for odd bargains in secondhand furniture shops and would buy more things if only you knew how to renovate them successfully. In either case I hope you will find this book just what you need to give you the confidence to tackle some of the simpler upholstery jobs yourself.

Most upholstery repair is largely a matter of common-sense and is not really difficult to do. It can be time-consuming and fiddly, but once the basic procedures are known, they can be applied to a great many different types of furniture. The main things you need plenty of are patience and space to work. When you take the webbing, springs and padding out of an old armchair it does make rather a lot of untidy mess on the floor, and this can be a bit daunting at first sight. The chances are that you will also have to leave the chair at times during the course of the work, perhaps for several days at a time. It does help a great deal, therefore, if you have a spare room, or a garage or somewhere you can work where it is possible to shut the door and forget all about it for a while until you have time to resume work again.

It is best to start by upholstering something fairly simple, like a dining chair with a drop-in seat, or a plain padded piano stool; then as you gain more confidence you can move on to the larger and more ambitious projects. A word of caution here though, about antique furniture. If you have valuable antiques which need re-upholstering, it is always best to take them to a professional upholsterer. Unless you are really sure of your skill and knowledge you might easily damage them in some way and reduce their value, so it is well worth paying to get them done properly. This caution also applies to a certain extent in the choice of fabrics. The appearance of a very attractive old piece of furniture can be spoiled by covering it in an unsuitable·modern fabric.

In the following pages I have described in step-by-step stages how to upholster, or re-upholster a wide range of furniture, from very simple items needing only to be re-covered, to rather more complicated things which need complete renovation. In most cases I have tried to show examples of furniture styles which are fairly common, so that although your dining chair may not be exactly the same as the one shown in this book, the basic method of construction is the same and you should be able to follow the instructions easily. Wherever possible I have used the original padding, springs etc., since the character and shape of most items is largely formed by the nature of their padding. This is not always possible, however, since old fillings may have deteriorated with age, and so I have included a section on polyether and latex foams which can be used to replace traditional fillings.

Tools and equipment

Most simple upholstery jobs can be tackled using the sort of tools that most people have around the house anyway. Other tools and aids can be improvised or home-made from offcuts of wood etc, but a few you will probably have to buy specially for the job. These can be kept to a minimum, though, and they can be bought one at a time as and when you need them so that the initial outlay will not be too great. Here is a list of some of the tools and equipment needed for different stages of the work:

PREPARING THE FRAME

REMOVING OLD NAILS AND TACKS: Professional upholsterers use a tool known as a *ripping chisel* for prising up studs and tacks, but this can easily be done with a *screwdriver* or an *old wood chisel*. The blade of the tool is placed against the tack and the handle is given a sharp tap with a *mallet*, this loosens the tack so that it can easily be prised out of the wood. Do not use a good chisel for this or you will absolutely ruin the cutting edge. Some of the longer tacks and nails may need a pair of *pincers* to pull them right out, and in some cases you can use the claw end of a small *claw-hammer* for this, but take care not to bruise or scratch the frame in the process. Where staples have been used to hold fabric etc. in place they can be removed with a screwdriver and pincers, but if there are a lot of them it is well worth investing in a *staple-remover*. There are several different types, and sometimes a *staple-tacker* will have one built into it somewhere.

MINOR REPAIRS TO FURNITURE FRAMES: If the furniture you plan to upholster is fairly old, it may have been re-covered several times and so may have a great many tack holes in the frame. These are best filled in with a *synthetic wood filler* which can be purchased in various different colours to tone in with the colour of the wood. Old furniture also often has wobbly legs and backs and sometimes tends to creak and squeak when in use. This is generally because the glue which holds the joints in place has perished with age. The easiest way to remedy this is to take the frame apart at the joints, scrape off all the old glue and substitute a modern *wood-working adhesive*, The frame should be re-assembled as quickly as possible once the adhesive has been applied, and should be cramped or bound in position whilst it is drying. Woodworkers *sash cramps* are best to use, but as they are fairly expensive to buy you can improvise with strong cord or string made into a tourniquet as shown in diagram 1. Remember to cushion all the edges of the frame against the cutting edge of the string by inserting off-cuts of wood or hardboard between it and the frame. Make sure also that all right-angle joints are truly positioned before the adhesive has time to set, as once it has dried it is virtually impossible to break the join again without

Diagram 1

Making a tourniquet to hold the frame in position whilst the adhesive is drying.

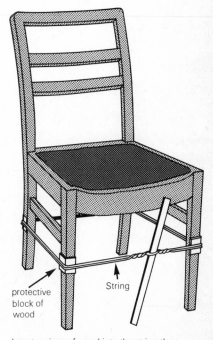

protective block of wood

String

Insert a piece of wood into the string then twist it to tighten up the string. Wedge the wood against the chair frame or the floor.

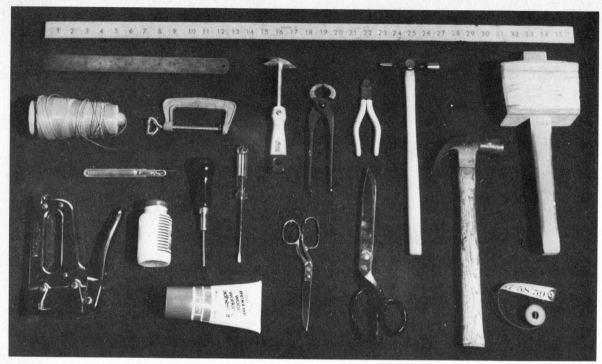

A selection of useful tools and adhesive

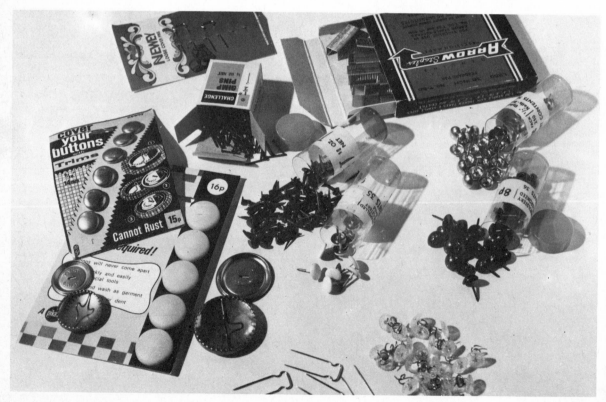

*A selection of nails, studs, tacks, loose cover pins,
twist pins, staples and button moulds*

6

serious damage to the furniture. Large cracks or splits in the frame can often be repaired in a similar way with adhesive, using smaller *G-cramps* to close up the wood while the adhesive is drying. Always examine the frame thoroughly for signs of woodworm and if this is prevalent treat it with a proprietary *woodworm killer* before re-upholstery. In older furniture you often find that woodworm is present in the inner parts of the frame which have not been stained or varnished, and do not show until you expose them by removing the padding etc.

For removing the old paint or varnish from a frame you can use one of the proprietary *paint strippers*, but if you have to tackle really ancient varnish, stripper can be more of a hindrance than a help and in cases where the varnish has become brittle with age it is far better to scrape it off dry. Where there is a lot of wood surface to treat, use a *combination shave-hook* which has specially shaped blades for getting into all the odd-shaped corners. For small areas a small, sharp-bladed *vegetable knife* can be used provided you are careful not to score the wood. When the paint or varnish has all been removed the wood should be rubbed down all over with *glasspaper*. This is available in a variety of grades but you should always finish off with a fine one for a really smooth surface. The type of stain, varnish, paint or polish you use for the frame once it is stripped is a matter of personal choice, but try to keep the surface of the frame in keeping with its age and style if you can.

HAMMERS AND OTHER TYPES OF TACK AND STAPLE INSERTERS: A small-headed hammer is necessary for inserting tacks and gimp pins into the frame. Special *upholsterers hammers* with magnetised heads can be obtained and these do save a lot of finger-hitting when you are using the very small types of tacks. Some of the upholsterers hammers have one end only magnetised, whilst the other end is clawed for removing the nails and tacks. Others are simply magnetised at one end and ordinary metal at the other, so that they can be used for inserting domed studs and larger nails. If you do not wish to buy a hammer specially, any small *tack hammer* can be used provided the head is small enough to allow you to insert tacks in confined corners and awkward places. A very useful tool to have is the *panel-pin or tack punch*, which is shaped rather like a screwdriver, but with a hollow shaft and a magnetised core. The tack is slipped, head first, into the hollow shaft where the head is drawn down on to the magnet. The punch is then pushed firmly against the area to be tacked and the shaft telescopes, pushing the tack firmly into the wood. On release the shaft springs back to its former length leaving the tack firmly embedded in the frame.

If you plan to do a lot of upholstering it is worth investing in a *staple-tacker*. This will save you a lot of time if you use it for holding lining and fabrics in place. Staples are not particularly attractive to look at though, so they should only be used on areas which will be covered by braid, or otherwise will not show on the finished article. A heavy-duty tacker is the best type to use, but you do need a good strong hand to depress the lever and care must always be taken to keep the base of the tacker flush with the surface of the wood frame while you insert the staple. The tacker has a tendency to jump away from the frame when the spring is depressed unless it is really firmly held.

TACKS, STUDS AND STAPLES: There are two main types of upholstery tacks, improved and fine. *Fine tacks* are used mainly for holding covering fabric and lining in place whilst *improved tacks*, which are thicker and stronger, are used for some of the heavier fabrics and for webbing

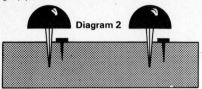

Placing a stud over the top of a tack or gimp pin to hide it.

Diagram 2

Webbing clips for rubber webbing.

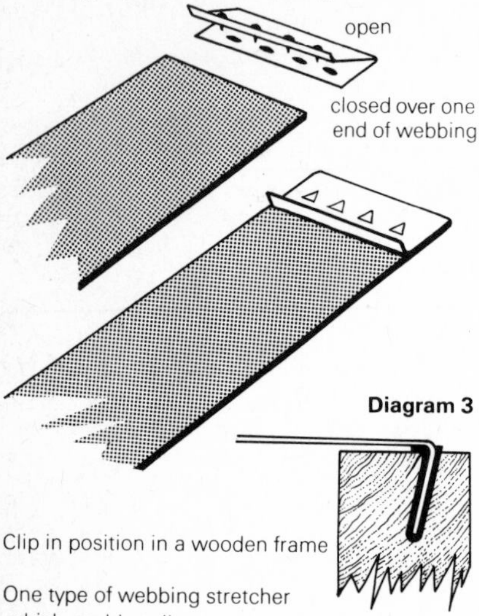

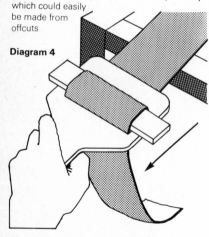

open

closed over one end of webbing

Diagram 3

Clip in position in a wooden frame

One type of webbing stretcher which could easily be made from offcuts

Diagram 4

Using a block of wood to stretch the webbing.

Diagram 5

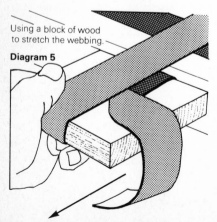

and hessian. Both types are made in various lengths from $\frac{1}{4}$ in. (6mm) to $\frac{5}{8}$ in. (15mm) and should be chosen according to the weight of the cloth and the thickness of the frame. *Gimp pins* are neater in appearance than tacks and have smaller heads so that they are less conspicuous. They are used for holding fabric and gimp or braid in place and are made in a variety of colours to tone in with the fabric. *Upholstery studs* are dual purpose; they are used for securing braid or fabric and they also form a decorative edging. They can be obtained in a variety of finishes such as brass, bronze, gunmetal and various different coloured enamels. Care must be taken when using studs not to chip the enamel or break off the head, this is easily done by catching the domed head a glancing blow with the hammer. Because of this danger, tacks are sometimes used to hold the fabric in place and then the studs are placed over them as shown in diagram 2 so that they form a decorative edging without taking any strain. Different sized *staples* are used with a staple-tacker, and the ones you choose will depend on the weight of cloth and the thickness of the frame. Avoid using staples which are too long, especially on hard wood, or they will simply stand up above the surface of the cloth and you will have to flatten them with a hammer. Also avoid using any which are too short or they will not hold the cloth securely. Staples are not generally suitable for holding webbing in place.

WEBBINGS, SPRINGS AND FILLINGS

WEBBINGS: The purpose of webbing in upholstery is to support the springs and/or padding in the seats and backs of furniture. There are three main types of webbing, *plain jute, coloured jute* and *black and white linen*. Coloured jute webbing is used mainly for binding carpets and it is not really strong enough to use on furniture. Plain brown jute webbing is thicker and stronger and is available in different widths for different purposes. Black and white linen webbing is the best quality. It is much stronger and more durable than jute and can easily be recognised by its distinctive herringbone-pattern weave. These webbings are used in conjunction with springs and the traditional types of padding, but in a lot of modern furniture *rubber webbing* is used to support cushions of latex or polyether foam. Rubber webbing is secured to the frame under tension; it can be fixed to the frame with long tacks or nails or with special *webbing clips*. When it is fixed in place with tacks or nails the ends of the webbing are not turned over as they are on the woven types since they will not fray. Three tacks are required at each end of each length. The special clips for attaching rubber webbing to wooden frames are slipped on to the ends of the pre-cut webbing and then closed in a vice, where the teeth of the clips hold the webbing in place. The clips are then slotted into angled rebates in the frame as shown in diagram 3. Special clips are also available for fitting this type of webbing to a metal frame. A five to ten per-cent stretch is necessary, and all lengths should be measured and cut accurately before attaching them to the frame. When woven jute or linen webbing is attached to a wooden frame it is not pre cut. A single hem is turned over on one end and this is tacked to the frame. Then a webbing stretcher is used to pull the webbing really taut before securing the other end. *Webbing stretchers* (diagram 4) can be bought but you will find a block of wood just as easy to use. Wrap the webbing around this as shown in diagram 5 and use it to lever against the frame until the webbing is really taut. Insert the tacks and then cut off the surplus webbing, not too near the tacks though, in case it frays.

SPRINGS: In older types of seating individual *coiled springs* were generally used between the webbing and the top padding. When the seats of old chairs and settees begin to sag in the middle it is usually either because the webbing has given way, or because the springs have shifted inside the seat. These springs have to be taken out, the webbing replaced with new, and the springs put back in again and sewn to the webbing. Step by step stages showing how to do this are given in the nursing chair on p.54. Occasionally webbing can be renewed in the base of a chair without removing the padding and springs.

Some modern types of seating have *tension springs* across the seat, and these are used in the same way as rubber webbing. Where they are incorporated into a fully upholstered seat they are usually left bare, but if they are to be covered only by a loose cushion they are often coated in a plastic skin to prevent damage to the cushion. This type of spring can be fixed to the frame with nails or with a special metal plate.

TRADITIONAL FILLINGS: These days, furniture is usually padded mainly with latex or polyether foam, but the older items will still have the traditional fibre fillings. The most widely used of these is *Coir fibre* which comes from the husk of the coconut. This was used mainly for the lower layers of padding, on top of the springs or webbing, and is usually covered by a layer of softer material which prevents the coir from penetrating the covering fabric. Coir fibre is sometimes loosely laid in the seat, or it can be made into fibre pads with a hessian base. *Hair* is another filling which is not often used these days due to its expense and the skill needed to use it properly. Although the term horshair is generally used, hair fillings can be made from the hair of cattle and other animals. Sometimes a seat is filled with a padding of *wood wool* as shown in the nursing chair on p.54. This is a cheap filling and needs a good layer of something softer on top to compensate for its rather coarse character. Top paddings can be made from a variety of materials. In old furniture you will often find a sort of *flock* made from shredded rags, this makes a firm surface but care must be taken if you remove it from the frame to keep it all in one piece and disturb it as little as possible or it may go lumpy and break up. *Kapok* is often used as the top layer of filling over the other types. This comes from the East Indies and is a vegetable fibre similar to cotton. It is very soft and light in weight but does tend to fly about a bit when you use it and clings to clothes and hair. A *wadding* in sheet form is often used as the topmost layer, this is simply cut to shape and size and laid over the other paddings to give a smooth outline. You can obtain both cotton and Terylene wadding by the yard. The Terylene type is usually rather thicker than the cotton one. *Polyester fibrefill* is a fairly new type of filling, it is extremely soft and resilient and can be used by itself in loose cushions or as an outer or top filling. It does not fly about when you use it as kapok does. *Feathers* and *down* are used as fillings for the more expensive types of furniture. They are very luxurious and are used mainly for loose cushions. They should always be enclosed in a down-proof calico cover inside the main outer cover.

DIFFERENT TYPES OF FOAM: As foam of one sort or another is used so extensively in modern furniture upholstery it is important to know what kind to use for each kind of job in order to obtain the best results. There are two main types. *Latex foam* which is made from natural latex, the sap of the rubber tree, and *Polyether foam* which consists mainly of by-products of the petrol industry and other chemicals.

Latex foam is often considered to be superior to Polyether. It is very resilient and has a softer feel but is usually heavier in weight. It does not have a very high tensile strength though, and must be protected from strong sunlight or it tends to crumble. This type of foam is supplied as moulded cushions, as sheets of varying thickness or in block form, which is then cut to the desired shapes and sizes. Sheet latex foam is divided again into three kinds: *Cavity sheet* which is between 1 inch (25mm) and 4 inches (10cm) thick and has largish cavities on one side; *pin-core* which has pencil-size holes on both sides and plain *sheet foam* which is up to 1 inch (25mm) thick with a smooth skin on both sides.

Polyether foam is supplied in block form in varying densities, and priced in relation to its density. When buying, it is a good idea to tell the retailer exactly what you want it for so that he can advise you on the best density to buy. It is not wise to choose a polyether foam in a lower density than has been recommended, as with constant use it will soon begin to sag and spoil the look and comfort of the furniture. The base on which the cushion is to be put will also govern the type of foam to use and its thickness. A wooden or other solid base will need a thick cushion for maximum comfort whilst a rubber webbing or tension spring base can have a much thinner one.

Foam converters, who buy foam direct from the manufacturers and cut it to size for the furniture industry, will also cut specific shapes and sizes for the retail customer. They will give estimates of the cost if told the exact measurements and the purpose to which the foam will be put. The advantages of using foam as an upholstery material are that it can be cut to any shape and will hold that shape provided the correct density is used. It is also generally lighter in weight than most of the traditional upholstery paddings and makes furniture easier to move about.

LINING FABRICS, THREAD AND TWINE

Hessian is a fairly open-weave coarse fabric made from jute fibre. It is natural grey/brown in colour with a slight fleck, and is extremely strong. Although it will not tear easily it does tend to fray rather a lot and because of its open weave it should always be tacked in place through a double thickness. The best way to do this is to fold over a single hem around the edges before tacking them down. Hessian is used mainly between the springs and the padding as a cover to prevent any of the filling from dropping down between the springs. It is also used as a dust-cover on the undersides of chair and settee seats, and sometimes also as a casing for fillings such as coir fibre. In order to save on expensive furnishing fabrics, strips of hessian are often sewn to the fabric and used as extensions to the cover where they will not show, for example down the back of the seat of an armchair. *Scrim* is very similar to hessian, being made from jute but with a more open weave which has a flat look to the threads. It is used to make casing for various loose fillings. *Calico* is made from closely woven unbleached cotton. It is a creamy colour with a brownish fleck and is made in several different thicknesses and widths. It is extremely useful for lining cushions, covering the tops of seats prior to covering them in upholstery fabric and for enclosing latex and polyether foam shapes to prevent them from feeling clammy. Strips of calico are often used to secure foam to a base. Unbleached calico does shrink rather a lot, so if you intend to use it for something which will need to be washed later on it is a good idea to pre-shrink it before use. In order to get square shapes true it is best to tear calico rather than cut it, and to pull the grain straight before sewing or tacking it in place.

For sewing calico linings ordinary *cotton thread* is suitable, and this can also be used for most natural furnishing fabrics made from cotton, linen or wool. Synthetic fabric though must be stitched with a *synthetic thread* and these are available in various thicknesses to suit the weight of the fabric. For heavier jobs such as stitching on buttons a *thin twine* should be used, and for sewing springs to webbing use a thicker twine. It is a good idea to wax thread and twine before using it by drawing it through a lump of *beeswax* or the stub of an old *candle*. This helps it to slide easily through the fabric or padding and also serves to some extent to protect it from wear.

There are several useful types of needle you can buy especially for upholstery work, the main ones being mattress needles, buttoning needles and sacking needles. The *mattress needle* is crescent shaped and is used for stitching corners and places which are difficult to get at. It is produced in various sizes for different types of fabric. The *buttoning needle* is very long and has a point at both ends. It is used wherever you have to stitch through thick layers of padding, particularly when you are sewing on buttons. The *sacking needle* is a large general-purpose one. It has a curved point for getting into awkward places and is useful for stitching springs to webbing and hessian. It should not be used for the covering fabric though, as it is rather thick and would make unsightly, large holes in the fabric. Another type of needle you will find useful is a *large darner* for stitching corners which are easy to reach and where you will find a straight needle easier to manage than a curved mattress needle.

SOME DIFFERENT TYPES OF UPHOLSTERY FABRIC

The two main points to bear in mind when choosing fabrics for upholstery are the suitability of the cloth with regard to the style and age of the furniture, and the wear and tear it is likely to get during use. With regard to the style of the furniture, you must also take into account the colour of the wood and also the surroundings it will eventually be placed in. Carvings and other embellishments on the frame should be echoed if possible in the design of the fabric, or a plain fabric should be chosen to enhance them. Many people make the mistake of covering dining chairs, regardless of age and style, with regency-stripe fabric, which looks fine on a Regency chair in a period setting, but does not really look good on a modern chair set in a contemporary room. These days there is a wide range of fabrics available in such a choice of colours and designs that you should always be able to find one which really compliments the piece of furniture. As far as the hard-wearing properties are concerned, your choice will depend on the amount of wear the furniture is likely to get. If you have a large energetic family of children and pets your sofa will need a tougher cover than it would if you have one quiet child and no pets. The fact that a fabric is tough and hard-wearing does not mean that it must be dull. Modern synthetic fibres and advances in dyeing and weaving techniques, together with mass-production have brought well-made, attractive fabrics within the reach of everyone. Always choose a good-quality upholstery fabric. Never use one which is intended for other purposes, such as dressmaking, since they are not designed to take the wear, and all your hard work will soon begin to look shoddy and worn.

It is impossible to list all the different types of upholstery fabrics here but I give below a brief description of some of the more well-known types. The names of the fabrics refer to their type of weave, not the fibre they are made from, so you should always enquire what the composition of the fabric is when you buy it so that you will know the type of thread to use and how best to tackle stains and general cleaning.

Brocade is a jacquard fabric with an intricately woven pattern in several colours. Originally it was made from silk, but nowadays can be cotton, wool or man-made fibres. *Brocatelle* is similar to brocade but the figured pattern is raised in shallow relief. *Corduroy* is a ribbed fabric with a cut pile similar to velvet. It is usually made from cotton, sometimes with the addition of a man-made fibre. It is very hard wearing and has a nap or one way pile so pattern pieces must all be cut with the pile running in the same direction. *Chintz* is a printed cotton fabric with a close weave and a glazed surface. It is generally used for loose covers, bedspreads and curtains. *Cretonne* is similar to chintz but lacks the glazed surface. *Damask* has a jacquard weave similar to brocade, but is reversible. It is often made from linen for use as table napkins and cloths, but heavier types are made from cotton, wool and man-made fibres. *Denim* is an inexpensive cotton fabric which is extremely hard wearing. It is usually produced in a few traditional plain colours but recently denims with a woven motif have been developed. Most *Leather* for upholstery is supplied as hides or half hides, a hide being the skin of the larger bovine animals such as cows and horses. It is expensive and because of its irregular shape can be wasteful if not cut out carefully. Upholstery with leather is a skilled job and should not be undertaken by beginners. *Linen-union* is a very tough mixture of linen and cotton with a printed design. Linen-union is often used for loose covers because it is washable, but allowance must be made for shrinkage. The printed designs are often traditional. *Moquette* both cut and uncut can be obtained. Uncut moquette has a pile of little loops all over it whilst cut moquette has a short pile similar to velvet. This type of fabric is extremely hard wearing but not very fashionable these days. *P.V.C. Coated fabrics* are divided into two main types, expanded and unexpanded. The unexpanded types are usually made on a woven cotton backing. Sometimes the cotton is printed with a design and clear P.V.C. is used to coat it. Sometimes a plain, undyed fabric is given a coating of coloured P.V.C. The expanded fabrics are usually made on a knitted instead of a woven backing and the coating is treated so that tiny bubbles of air are trapped in it to make it thicker. Expanded P.V.C. fabric is usually plain-coloured but often has an embossed, creased pattern on its surface to imitate leather. P.V.C. stands for Polyvinyl chloride. *Repp* is a hard wearing plain woven fabric which is fairly inexpensive. It is usually made from cotton in a wide range of plain colours. *Sateen* has a characteristic smooth surface made by the weft threads which are long and run across the surface of the warp threads. It can be plain or printed. *Satin* is similar to sateen but it is the warp threads which form the smooth surface. Both satin and sateen can be made from a wide range of different fibres. *Tapestry* is usually expensive. It is a jacquard fabric traditionally made from wool in complicated colours and weaves. *Tweed* can be made from wool or from other fibres. It has a simple weave, often incorporating different, toning colours and is priced in relation to its weight and the fibres it is made from. *Velvet* was originally made from silk, but these days is more often cotton or synthetic fibres. It has a luxurious pile with a definite one way nap, so cutting out must be planned carefully. Dralon velvet is becoming extremely popular as an upholstery fabric because of its qualities of stain and crush resistance. This is made from acrylic fibre which can be dyed in a wide range of both bright and subtle colours. *Velveteen* is similar to velvet but usually has a coated backing to keep the pile anchored in place.

BRAIDS, FRINGINGS AND OTHER TRIMMINGS

There is a wide range of upholstery trimmings on the market and a visit to the haberdashery departments of one or two large stores should prove rewarding. The choice of trimmings will of course depend on the type of furniture and fabric you have chosen. Generally speaking though, *flat braids* are used to cover the raw edges of fabric where they are attached to a frame and the braid usually matches or tones in with the colour of the fabric. *Fringing* is sometimes used around the lower edges of items such as arm-chairs or sofas, whilst some of the more elaborate jacquard fabrics look best trimmed with an ornate braid that is *tasselled* or has a thick crinkly pile. If you have difficulty in matching the braid to the colour of the fabric you can try matching it to the colour of the wood, or where the fabric is patterned you can pick out one of the colours in the design as I have done with the chaise longue shown on p.60. Braid can either be stuck on with a fabric adhesive or tacked in place with gimp pins or studs.

You can sometimes buy *ready-made pipings* instead of making your own as shown on p.18. The manufactured ones usually consist of a flat braid with one edge thickened and often corded. They are used in the same way as hand-made piping, the flat part being sandwiched between the seams and the corded edge providing the decoration.

Buttons: The type of cover-it-yourself *button moulds* used by dress-makers are suitable for upholstery, particularly the plastic and metal ones. These always have the instructions on how to cover them printed on their card. It is also possible to buy ready-made buttons covered usually in P.V.C. fabric, but these have the disadvantage that they do not always match up with the colour of fabric you intend to use.

Furniture
with a solid base

If you have never tackled any upholstery before, try to start with something which has a solid base like the patchwork piano stool shown below. This stool would be very easy for a beginner to re-cover because its solid base should have prevented any loss of padding and there is no webbing or springs to contend with. Some dining chairs with drop-in seats also have this type of plywood base and are tackled in much the same way, except that the fabric is tacked to the underside of the seat instead of the sides. Seats like this usually have a flock padding with a top layer of kapok or wadding and sometimes a base of coir fibre. If the padding is in really bad shape you can easily add extra to it and build it up again. The solid base gives you a firm foundation to build on. A calico lining is a great help too, since if you cannot get the padding really smooth the first time you can place a layer of wadding over the calico lining before you put the main cover on. This is really cheating though, and you should try to get a good shape before putting on the lining. Once you have tackled a seat of this type you can see that the method can be applied to other things. For example, if you have a large wooden box with a hinged lid you can make it into a most attractive jewel box by covering the sides and base with a fabric, padding the lid to a domed shape with kapok and then covering this in a matching fabric. A neat braid trim around the base of the lid and a tassel at the front for lifting it, and you have a most attractive gift for someone. You could perhaps embroider the fabric for the lid before you put it on, or sew little beads on to it in a pattern, or make a patchwork of tiny shapes, whichever you prefer.

Patchwork Covered Piano Stool

Now that fewer people have a piano in the parlour, old piano stools are fairly easy to come by in secondhand furniture shops. Some of these are most attractive in their own right and make ideal bathroom or bedroom stools. The one shown here was bought very cheaply in an antique shop. It has a hinged, padded lid over a small tray for keeping sheet music, and I have found this very useful for storing tissues or hair rollers. The wooden frame of the stool was sound when it was bought, but the varnish had become a little scratched and chipped at some time and so it was decided to scrape off all the old varnish and stain, and to paint the woodwork white.

   This kind of stool is just the right size for showing off a small treasured piece of tapestry or patchwork, provided that the fabric chosen is strong enough to stand up to the wear it is likely to get. If you line the seat first with calico and then put the patchwork or tapestry on top of this you can remove the outer cover occasionally for cleaning and repair. If you make a patchwork with the idea of using it to upholster something like this remember to choose the same type of fibre for all the patches, i.e., all cotton or all wool; then you will not get into difficulty with uneven shrinkage or uneven wear. Another point to bear in mind is that the grain of the fabric must run in the same direction on all patches. This is because the cover is stretched fairly tightly over the cushion and if the grain is going the wrong way on some patches they may stretch out of shape or become wrinkled or puckered.

Since a stool like this has a solid plywood base to the cushion rather than a webbing one, the stuffing usually keeps fairly well to its original shape, but you may find that it has sunk a little in the centre and needs a little extra kapok to restore it to a good, full shape.

The materials you will need are as follows: Paint for the frame; extra kapok for padding; calico lining; gimp pins; a piece of embroidery, tapestry, patchwork or furnishing fabric; matching or toning braid trim; matching or toning enamelled upholstery studs.

METHOD

Undo the screws which secure the hinges to the lid; also remove the screws from the lid-stay if there is one. Lift off the lid of the stool and put all the small metal parts and screws safely aside to replace later on. Remove the old varnish from the wooden surfaces of the frame if necessary, either scraping it off dry or using a proprietary paint stripper, then filling in any bad scratches or chips with wood-filler. Sand down the frame all over with fine glasspaper and then paint it first with an undercoat and then a top-coat of paint in the colour of your choice.

Prise out all the tacks or studs holding the old cover in place and then remove it carefully from the lid and put it aside for later use. Carefully lift the padding from the wooden part of the lid. Remove the old varnish from the underside and side edges of the lid, fill in any chips or bad scratches, sand it smooth and apply undercoat and top-coat of paint to match the rest of the frame. Leave the frame and lid for about two days to dry so that the paint will have plenty of time to harden before you start re-padding the lid.

Press the old cover out flat and use it as a pattern for cutting out the calico lining. When the paint on the lid is thoroughly dry, replace the padding and examine it carefully to see if you will need any extra kapok to give it a good shape. If you do, arrange this on to the existing padding, shaping it into a gentle domed shape in the centre of the seat. If the padding is in really bad shape you can replace it entirely with a piece of foam attached with tape or calico strips as shown in diagram 5 on p.26. Do not use too thick a piece though. Try to make the seat about the same thickness and general shape as it was originally. When you are satisfied with the fullness and shape of the padding arrange the calico lining over it and secure this to the top edges of the lid with gimp pins. Take great care to pull the cover really taut all over and make the corners as smooth a fit as possible.

If you intend to make a piece of patchwork specially to fit the stool top, buy or make a suitable sized template in the shape you prefer and cut out the 'papers' from an iron-on interfacing such as Vilene. These will have to be really accurate or your shapes will not fit together correctly. Iron these shapes on to the wrong side of the chosen fabric, then cut out the fabric patches about $\frac{1}{2}$in. (12mm) larger all around than the interfacing. Turn down the hem allowance all round each shape and tack it in place. It is a good idea to measure your old cover to find out the exact size of patchwork needed, and then to make a

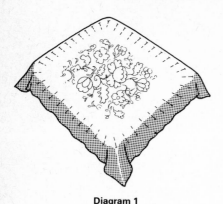

scale pattern of the arrangement of your different coloured shapes. Join your shapes with small, neat slipstitching on the wrong side, making sure to keep the grain running in the same direction on every one. Leave the tacking stitches in the work until it has been firmly attached to the stool top as they prevent the seams on the inside from becoming ruffled and causing bumpy patches in the finished cover.

Press the new cover carefully all over with a damp cloth and a medium-hot iron and then place it on to the stool lid and centre the design carefully. Pin the cover to the calico around the top of the cushion as shown in diagram 1, pulling it taut across the top of the cushion and keeping the centre of the design in the centre of the seat. Anchor the cover to the wooden frame temporarily with one or two tacks along each side, then permanently attach first one short end of the cover to the frame and then the other, pulling the fabric firmly all the time to avoid any wrinkles. When both ends are secured, do the centre section of each side, leaving about a third untacked at each end of each side. Once these centres are secured, work outwards from them to the corners, easing in the fabric as you go so that it fits smoothly and tightly over the corners. Trim off the surplus fabric from around the edges of the cover so that the braid trimming will cover the raw edges. If you are using patchwork, carefully remove all the tacking stitches, holding the seams in place and, if necessary, press the top of the stool with a medium-hot iron to remove the marks left by the tackings.

Cut a length of braid to go all around the edge of the seat and arrange it so that the join occurs at the hinged side of the stool. Attach this braid to the edges of the seat with upholstery studs spaced at regular intervals. Replace the seat on to the stool and replace the hinges and lid stay screws. If you wish you can attach a fabric or braid tab to the front edge of the seat to assist raising the lid. This helps to prevent soiling of the cover from constant handling.

Making Your Own Piping

Very often the edge of a cover needs to be clearly defined to give a good shape to the cushion inside and, where this is the case, piping is often the best way to show off the edge. Piping can also be used to strengthen the edges and corners and to provide a contrast or matching trim between two sections of a cover.

If you plan to make your own piping you must first estimate the length you will need, adding extra for shrinkage if you are using a cotton cord. Then decide how thick you want the piping to be. Both cotton and nylon piping cords are made in various thicknesses and should be selected in relation to the size of the furniture and the thickness of the fabric being used for the cover. The next thing to consider is whether you want the piping to match the covering fabric or to be in contrast to it, and whether you want it plain or patterned. If you are using a fabric such as a printed linen-union you may wish to cut out the strips for encasing the piping cord from the same fabric, or you may wish to pick out one of the colours in the design and pipe the cover in this. Where the piping will not get a great deal of wear you can use a purchased bias binding to enclose the cord, but for areas which will have to put up with constant wear and tear it is better to cut your own bias strips from something a bit more substantial.

To estimate how wide the strips will need to be, you will have to measure around the cord to see how much fabric it takes up, then add

Different types of upholstery fabrics (see page 10)

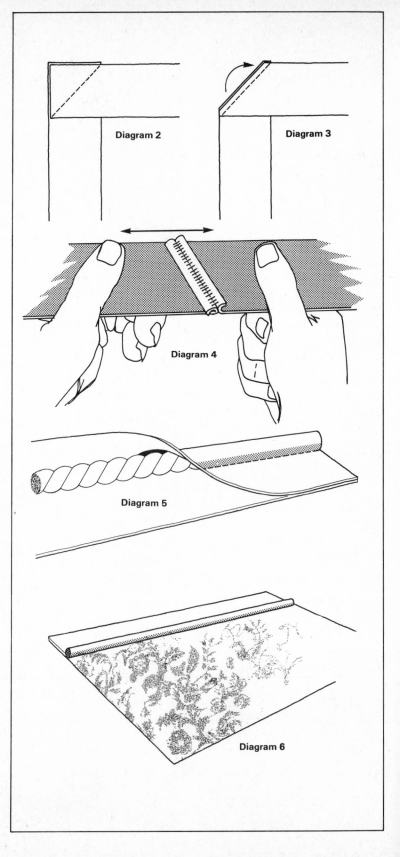

Diagram 2

Diagram 3

Diagram 4

Diagram 5

Diagram 6

on to this twice the seam allowance of the cover. The total measurement will be the width of the bias strip to be cut out. The strips are cut in the following way: Mark the fabric into a square and then fold one corner of this diagonally to the opposite corner. Press the diagonal fold of the fabric into a sharp crease with a warm iron. Then you can use this crease as your first cutting line and measure the widths of the strips from either side of this using a straightedge and tailors' chalk. Cut off as many strips as you need to make up the desired length. When all the strips are cut out they should be joined together with a seam on the wrong side as shown in diagram 2, then trim off the surplus fabric as shown in diagram 3 and iron the seam open as shown in diagram 4. If the piping cord you are using is a cotton one it will shrink considerably if it is washed, so if you are making a washable cover the cord should be pre-shrunk by washing and drying it thoroughly before you make up the piping.

Lay the fabric strip, wrong side up on the table, centre the cord on to it and then fold the strip over the cord as shown in daigram 5. Pin both sides together and then tack them as close to the cord as you can down the entire length of the piping. When you come to make up the cover, place the piping on the right side of the fabric with the raw edges together and the corded side facing in towards the centre of the fabric as shown in diagram 6. Where you have a curved seam or where you have to turn a sharp corner you can clip into the bias fabric as far as the tacking, but no further or the cut may show on the finished piping. When turning around curves or corners, be generous with the piping and squash it up a little so that it will stand out from the curve when the cover is turned right side out. If you skimp the piping around a curve it will be too tight and could pucker the fabric badly along the line of the seam.

Detachable Cover for a Pouffe

It is surprising the amount of difference a simple fabric cover can make to something like the pouffe shown here. The original covering was made from two different coloured plastics, bonded together at the seams. These had split at one side and the stuffing was showing plainly through the hole, so a patch was made from calico and stuck in place with adhesive, drawing the edges of the seams together to close them. The new cover is held in place by a draw-string running through a hem around its base so that it can easily be removed for cleaning. A finishing touch is given by piping the top edge of the cover in a contrast colour and then tying a length of matching dressing-gown cord around the middle of the pouffe to help keep its sides firmly in shape. The fabric chosen for the cover is a brightly coloured moquette with a rich design which is ideal for something as small as this but could look rather garish on a larger item.

The materials you will need are as follows: A small pouffe or solid footstall, enough furnishing fabric to cover it plus a generous lower hem allowance; enough piping cord and bias binding to go around the top edge of the cover; matching sewing thread; a length of dressing-gown cord to go twice around the girth of the pouffe; a fairly long piece of string or cord and a large safety pin or bodkin.

METHOD
Repair the old cover of the pouffe if necessary and remove the band

Braids, fringings and other trimmings (see page 13)

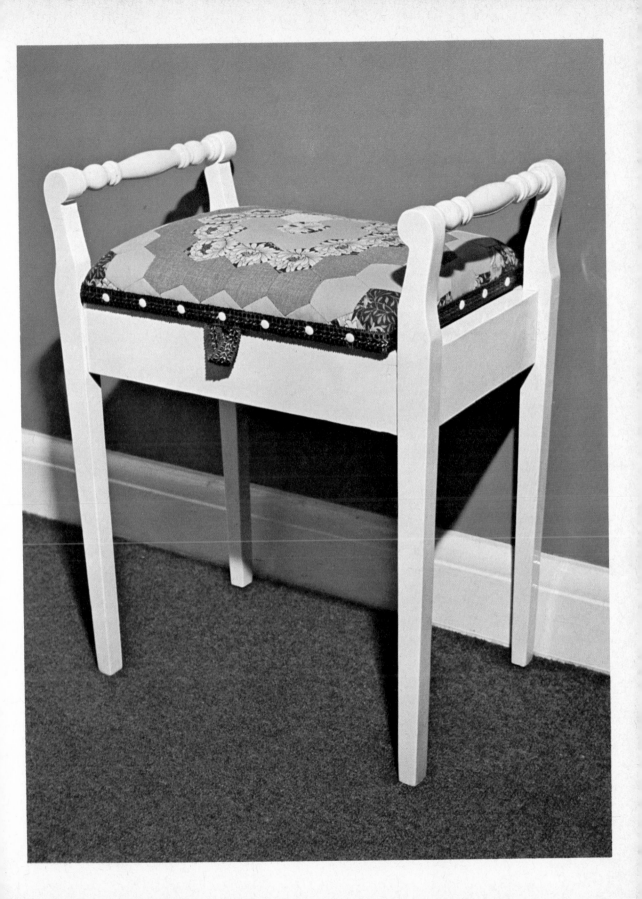

A patchwork-covered piano stool (see page 14)

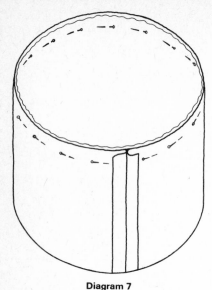

Diagram 7
Pinning piped top of cover to side section

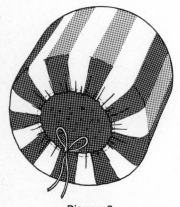

Diagram 8
Drawing up string to close base of cover.

from around its sides if there is one. Make a paper pattern $\frac{1}{2}$in. (12mm) larger all around than the top of the pouffe, using a compass to draw out the shape if it is a round one, or a ruler and set-square if it is a square or a rectangle. Measure around the sides of the pouffe and add on 1in. (25mm) to this measurement. Then measure the height from the top edge to the floor and add on 6in. (150mm). Cut out a rectangle of fabric to these two measurements and also a piece for the top of the cover using your paper pattern. Make up a length of piping to go around the top edge of the cover by pressing the bias binding out flat, placing the piping cord in the centre of it and re-folding the binding over the cord. Tack the two layers of binding together as close to the cord as possible to hold it firmly in place. Arrange the piping around the edges of the top section of the pouffe cover so that the corded edge is facing towards the centre and the line of tacking stitches is $\frac{1}{2}$in. (12mm) from the raw edges. Neaten both edges of the piping where they join, then pin and tack it in place all around. Machine stitch the piping to the cover using a piping foot and stitching as close to the cord as possible. Take the rectangle of fabric and with right sides facing, join the two sides together with a $\frac{1}{2}$in. (12mm) seam; press the seam open. With right sides facing, insert the piped top of the cover into the top of the side section taking care to see that the fabric design, or pile if there is one, is facing the right way up, and placing the side seam level with the join in the piping. Pin the top in place all around as shown in diagram 7, easing in the edges where necessary for a smooth fit. Tack in place all around and then machine the seam, using a piping foot and stitching as close to the piping cord as possible. Trim the seam to about $\frac{1}{4}$in. (6mm) and overcast it all around to prevent fraying. Turn up a $1\frac{1}{2}$in. (38mm) single hem around the open end of the cover and stitch in place 1in. (25mm) from the folded edge. Overcast the raw edge of the fabric around this hem if it looks as though it will fray. Turn the cover right side out and insert the pouffe into it, pushing it firmly in and taking care to see that the top and side seams are lying flat inside the cover. Cut a piece of string or cord about 4in. (10cm) longer than the length of the lower hemmed edge and then thread this on to the safety pin or bodkin. Starting at the side seam, thread it through the lower hem. Arrange the string so that 2in. (5cm) of each end protrudes from the base of the side seam, then tie these two ends together in a single knot and draw them up tightly. Arrange the gathers evenly around the hem as shown in diagram 8 and pull up the string as tightly as you can. Then tie the ends into a bow and tuck them inside the base of the cover. When you come to remove the cover for cleaning, take care not to pull the string out of its casing so that you will not have to thread it in again when you replace the cover.

Using latex and polyether foams

Foam can be shaped for all sorts of cushions and paddings and is especially suitable for use on solid-based items such as stools and storage boxes. A *latex adhesive* should be used to stick various sections together and you can make up quite complicated shapes in this way. Because of its resilience foam can also be pulled or pushed into any particular shape of cover and shape can also be governed by how this is attached to the foam. When using latex adhesive it is best to lightly coat both surfaces to be joined and, when the adhesive has almost dried, press them gently together. This type of joining must be done accurately though, since it is very difficult to pull the sections apart again without tearing the foam. If you accidentally spill some adhesive on to a section which does not need to be glued, or if you use too much adhesive, the surplus can be neutralised by dusting it lightly with *talcum powder* or *French chalk*.

Cutting out rectangles and squares from foam presents no difficulty if you use a *metal ruler* or other *straightedge* as a guide. Take care to keep the knife blade at right-angles to the surface of the foam and thus avoid undercutting. An old *breadknife* is an ideal tool for cutting foam, particularly the type which has a *hollow ground* blade and, if you have trouble drawing it through the foam, try dipping it into water occasionally to help it to slide. Rounded or irregular shapes are a little more difficult to cut out and the best way to tackle these is as follows: Make two identical *templates* of the shape to be cut, pierce a hole through the centre of each one, then place one template on each side of the foam and thread them both together through the pierced holes with strong twine. Draw the twine up and tie it really tightly. Then work the knife around the edges of both the templates, cutting through the foam which is sandwiched between them. Use a long-bladed knife for this. Remove the templates and you will have a shape with clean-cut sides all around. Thin sheet foam can usually be cut with *large scissors* or a sharp *craft knife*, but take care to keep the angle of the cut consistent throughout to avoid getting ragged or oblique edges.

Handbuilding is the term given to the building up of shapes from several pieces of foam. Even a plain square cushion will be improved if you make it slightly domed in the centre so that its cover is kept taut and thus prevented from becoming puckered. Making a domed shape like this is very simply done by sandwiching a small piece of foam between two larger pieces as shown in diagram 1 and the gluing the two outer layers together around the edges. The same principal applies to furniture with a solid base such as the ottoman shown on p.30, but here the small piece of foam is stuck directly on to the lid of the chest and then the larger piece is placed over it and stuck down to the edges of the lid. To round the edges of a shallow cushion on a

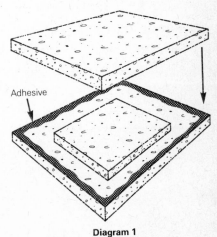

Adhesive

Diagram 1
Making a domed cushion by
the insertion of a centre piece.

A pouffe with detachable cover (see page 19)

P.V.C.-covered kitchen stool cushions (see page 26)

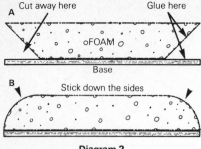

Diagram 2
Making a shallow, domed cushion
on a solid base.

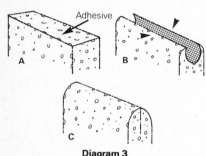

Diagram 3
Compressing a straight edged to make it rounded.

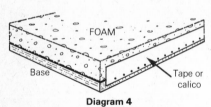

Diagram 4
Attaching cushion to base with tape or calico
for easy removal.

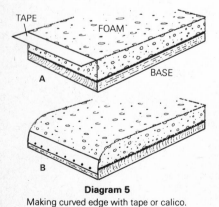

Diagram 5
Making curved edge with tape or calico.

solid base you can undercut them as shown in diagram 2 (A & B) and then stick them to the base, using a strip of calico. Make sure your foam is slightly larger all around than the base, to allow for some fullness over the curved edge.

If you want to make a cushion without a gusseted edge, a rounded effect can be obtained by spreading a little adhesive on to the side edges of the foam and then, when this has become tacky, pressing them carefully together as shown in diagram 3 (A, B & C). This type of cushion looks best with a simple two-piece cover and a piped seam around the curved edges.

When you plan to secure a cushion to a solid base consider first of all whether you will want to remove it again at any time. If not, you can simply stick it down around the edges with latex adhesive. If, however, you want the cushion removable, the best way of attaching it is with a strip of calico or a length of wide tape. This is stuck to the side of the cushion with adhesive and then tacked to the edges of the base with upholstery tacks as shown in diagram 4. This method can also be used to make curved edges to the cushion by sticking the calico strip to the top edge of the foam and then pulling it down to the base as shown in diagram 5 (A & B).

P.V.C. Covered Stool Cushions

Plain wooden kitchen stools can be rather hard and unyeilding to sit on unless they have some sort of padded cushion to give them a little extra comfort. A plain tailored cover over a shaped foam cushion will greatly improve both the comfort and the looks of this type of stool and is very easy to make.

A P.V.C. coated cotton fabric is ideal as a cover for a kitchen or breakfast room stool because it can easily be wiped over with a damp cloth to remove any marks or spills. The offcuts of fabric can be used to make simple place mats to match the stools and you will then have an attractive breakfast bar ensemble. The piping around the top edge of the cushion helps to keep it in shape and as the foam inside is cut out slightly larger all around than the top of the stool, it fills the cover tightly and dispels any large wrinkles in the cover. To create a slightly domed effect an offcut of thin sheet foam has been placed centrally under the main cushion shape as described on p.23. There is no need to line this type of cushion with calico first. The main cover can go straight over the foam and the studs will hold it firmly in place.

When sewing a fabric like P.V.C. with a sewing machine, the machine should be set to a fairly large stitch, a good sharp needle must be used and you should always try stitching on an offcut first so that you can adjust the thread tension as necessary. For some sewing machines you can obtain a special presser foot for sewing leather and P.V.C. This has a small roller instead of the normal flat plate, and this helps the fabric to roll smoothly under the needle instead of clinging to the underside of the foot plate. If you cannot get one of these for your machine, you can use a piece of greaseproof or tissue paper, placed over the fabric to shield it from the foot. Stitch right through the paper and tear it away from the stitching when you have finished. Always clean your machine thoroughly after using it to stitch a P.V.C. fabric, especially around the bobbin and shuttle-race. Little particles of the plastic coating can get down into the mechanism and may cause it to jam if they are left to accumulate.

The materials for this type of stool cushion are as follows: A wooden kitchen stool, round or oval; A piece of 2in. (5cm) thick polyether foam at least the size of the stool top, plus 1in. (25mm); Sufficient P.V.C. coated cotton fabric for the top of the stool and a 3½in. (9cm) wide gusset; matching sewing thread; clear, household adhesive; sufficient piping cord to go around the top of the stool; coloured enamel upholstery studs to match the fabric.

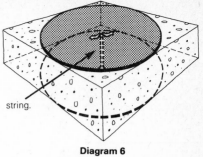

Using double template to cut out a foam shape.

string.

Diagram 6
Kitchen Stool

METHOD

To make the pattern for the stool top, turn the stool upside down on to a sheet of newspaper and draw around the top. Remove the stool and cut out the newspaper ½in. (12mm) larger all around than the drawn shape. Make two card templates from this pattern and pierce a hole in the centre of each. (Diagram 6). Place one template on either side of your sheet of foam and tie them tightly together through the centre holes with strong thread or thin twine. Now cut out the foam circle or oval using a very sharp breadknife or similar type of knife and using the edges of the two templates as a guide at either side of the foam. If you have difficulty in drawing the knife through the foam, dip it occasionally into water to help it to slide. Cut out a circle of P.V.C. fabric ½in. (12mm) larger all round than the card template and then measure around the sides of the stool top and cut a strip of fabric 1in. (25mm) longer than this measurement and 3½in. (9cm) wide. Also cut a bias strip of the fabric the same length as the gusset but 1½in. (38mm) wide for the piping.

Place the piping cord down the centre of the wrong side of this bias strip, then fold the strip in half over the cord and stick both sides firmly together with adhesive. Leave this to dry thoroughly. Take the wider, gusset strip and join both short ends with a ½in. (12mm) seam, open the seam out flat and stick it down with adhesive. Position the piping strip around one long side of the gusset, on the right side with the raw edges together, then stick it in place sparingly with the adhesive, keeping this within the seam allowance. Join the two ends of the piping neatly, level with the side seam of the gusset. Clip into the seam allowance of the fabric circle at about ½in. (12mm) intervals all around, then insert this into the piped side of the gusset strip with right sides facing and the piping sandwiched between the gusset and the circle. Ease the edges of the circle into place so that it fits the gusset smoothly. Use clothes pegs or small bulldog clips to hold it in place whilst you arrange it and then stick the sections together within the seam allowance, using the adhesive sparingly.

If your sewing machine will cope with the four thicknesses of the P.V.C. fabric, use a piping foot and stitch the top seam, as close to the piping cord as possible, all around. If you have trouble with the machine you can stitch the seam by hand, using a large glover's needle and strong linen thread. Make short stab-stitches through the fabric and pull the thread taut but not tight enough to make puckers. Turn up a ½in. (12mm) hem around the lower edge of the gusset and stick this in place with adhesive. Turn the cover right side out and insert the foam cushion into it, making sure that the seam allowance around the top edge of the cover is positioned so that it lies down flat around the sides of the foam. Cut a piece of thinner, sheet foam about 2in. (5cm) smaller all around than the top of the stool. Position this in the centre of the stool and stick it in place with adhesive. Place the main cushion on to the stool on top of this and pull the lower edges of the cover down so that they are level with the lower wooden edge of the stool

Ottoman and bolster (see page 30)

OPPOSITE Buttoned cushion for a wooden chair (see page 36)

seat. Place several tacks at intervals around the edge of the cover to hold it temporarily in place and then position the domed upholstery studs at regular intervals all around the lower edge of the stool seat to secure the cover permanently to the stool.

If you want to make matching place mats as shown in the photograph, simply cut out 11in. by 16in. (280mm by 406mm) rectangles, either plain-edged or with pinking shears. There is no need to hem P.V.C. coated fabric since it will not fray.

Braid-trimmed Ottoman and Bolster Cushion

It is very simple to make an attractive ottoman from an ordinary whitewood blanket chest. By covering the body of the chest in fabric and then making a cushion seat of the lid you can create an extremely functional and good-looking piece of bedroom furniture at a fraction of the price of a ready-made ottoman. If you line the inside in the way we have done here, attaching the lining only around the inside top of the chest, you will find it easy to remove blanket fluff, etc., from the bottom of the chest by simply turning out the lining in the same way you would turn out a trouser pocket.

Bolster cushions can be purchased filled with feathers or made from block polyether foam, or you can make your own by rolling up a sheet of thin foam like a swiss-roll and then securing the outside edge with latex adhesive. A 9in. (23cm) diameter bolster is a good size for the back of an ottoman, but you could use a smaller one if you prefer.

Provided your blanket chest is not more than 3ft 9in. (1 metre, 14cm) long and 1ft 9in. (54cm) wide you can estimate roughly the amount of fabric needed to cover it in the following way: Open the lid and measure the height of the chest (minus the lid) from the base up over the top edge and down inside the chest to a depth of about 4in. (10cm). Call this measurement A. Measure across the lid from front to back, add on 1in. (25mm), and call this measurement B. Multiply measurement A by three, add on measurement B, then add on a further 14in. (36cm) for the sides of the cushion and about 30in. (76cm) for the bolster. The total measurement will be the length of plain 48in. wide furnishing fabric you will need to buy.

If you are using a patterned fabric you may have to add on a little extra in order to match up the design. The amount will depend on the size of the design repeat and you should ask about this when purchasing the fabric. The main design should be placed centrally on the front and back of the chest, the centre of the lid and the centre of each end. Patterns should match up if possible on the lid, the front of the lid and the front of the chest. The lengthwise grain of both plain and patterned fabrics should run in the direction shown by the arrows on diagram 7.

The other materials you will need are as follows: Roughly the same amount of 48in. wide calico lining; a piece of 3in. (75mm) thick pincore foam about $\frac{1}{2}$in. (12mm) larger than the size of the lid; a piece of $\frac{1}{2}$in. (12mm) thick sheet foam about 3in. (75mm) smaller all around than this; a piece of $\frac{1}{2}$in. (12mm) thick sheet foam about 3in. (75mm) smaller again; a bolster cushion about 9in. (23cm) in diameter and as long as the chest lid; enough piping cord and 1in. (25mm) wide bias binding to go around the top of the chest lid and around each end of the bolster; enough fringed furnishing braid to go around the base of the chest;

Direction of the design if using a patterned fabric.

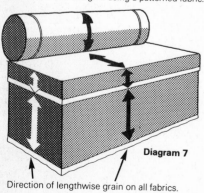

Diagram 7

Direction of lengthwise grain on all fabrics.

enough unfringed braid to go around the lower edge of the lid and around each end of the bolster; matching sewing thread; latex adhesive; gimp pins or small upholstery tacks.

METHOD

To cut out the fabric: Cut off three lengths to measurement A, cutting across the fabric from selvedge to selvedge and following the weave of the fabric. One of these is for the front, one for the back and the other one is divided in half for both ends of the chest. Cut a piece of fabric to measurement B, then measure the length of the chest lid from end to end and trim this piece of fabric to that length plus 1in. (25mm), removing equal amounts of the surplus fabric from each selvedge edge if the fabric is patterned in order to keep the design in the centre of the lid. Cut three $4\frac{1}{2}$in. (115mm) wide strips across the fabric from selvedge to selvedge to make the side edges of the cushion, then put the remainder of the fabric aside for the bolster cover. From the calico cut out a piece to measurement B and trim it to the length of the chest lid plus 1in. (25mm). Then cut three strips 4in. (10cm) wide for the cushion gusset. Put the rest aside for the lining.

To make up the cushioned lid: First remove the lid from the chest by unscrewing the hinges. It is a good idea to replace the screws in the lid in their original holes, so that they protrude slightly. Then you can prevent bulky seams from covering the screw holes and making life difficult when you come to replace the hinges. Put the lid, right side up on a bench or table and centre the smallest piece of sheet foam on to it. Stick this to the lid with latex adhesive, and when the adhesive has dried, place the next size piece of sheet foam on top and stick this in place. When the second lot of adhesive is dry, place the thick piece of foam on to the lid and stick it in place around all four sides. You now have a slightly domed cushion on the lid.

Join the three 4in. (10cm) strips of calico to make one continuous strip, then stitch this to the edges of the piece of calico which was cut to measurement B, making a $\frac{1}{2}$in. (12mm) seam. Clip into the seam allowance at the corners as you turn them as shown in diagram 8 in order to make a neat right-angled turn at each one. When you get almost round to where you started stitching you will be able to estimate how much surplus calico to trim from the end of the strip in order to join both ends with a neat $\frac{1}{2}$in. (12mm) seam. Press this seam open and then continue to join the strip to the rectangle to make a lining with a side gusset around all four sides. Press the lining well, pressing the seams down towards the gusset. Then turn it to the right side and place it over the cushioned lid. Smooth the cover evenly and tightly down over the cushion and tack the lower edges to the wooden lid temporarily with gimp pins at intervals. Arrange the cover so that about $\frac{1}{2}$in. (12mm) of the calico overlaps the top edge of the wood (to do this you will have to press down firmly on the edge of the cushion to squash it as you insert the tacks). When you are satisfied that the lining is correctly positioned, tack it in place permanently all around, taking care to get all the edges even and unwrinkled and hammering the tacks firmly home.

Make up the piping by pressing the bias binding open with a warm iron, inserting the cord in the centre, then re-folding the binding over the cord. Baste both sides of the binding together as close to the cord as possible. Arrange the piping around the edges of the rectangle of fabric which was cut to measurement B, placing it on the right side of the fabric with all the raw edges level and the cord facing in towards

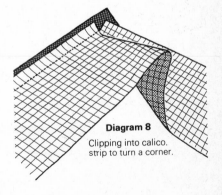

Diagram 8
Clipping into calico.
strip to turn a corner.

Buttoned cushion seat for a toy box (see page 37)

the centre of the rectangle. Clip into the corners of the binding as shown in diagram 9 so that it can be turned smoothly around the corners. Pin and tack the piping in place around all four sides of the rectangle, joining both ends carefully in the centre of one long side. Then machine-stitch in place using a piping foot on the machine and stitching as close to the cord as possible. Join the three 4½in. (115mm) strips of furnishing fabric to make one long strip, find the centre of this, and mark it with a pin. With right sides facing, pin the strip around the edges of the piped rectangle. Start in the centre of the long side opposite the joined piping, and position the centre of the strip here. Clip into the corners of the strip as you pin it to the rectangle in the same way as for the calico lining. Estimate the amount of strip you will need to trim away from each end in order to place the join level with the join in the piping. Then stitch the ends of the strip together with a ½in. (12mm) seam, press this open and continue pinning the strip to the side of the rectangle. Tack all the layers together all around and then machine stitch the seam as close to the cord as possible, using a piping foot. Trim the seam if and where necessary and overcast the edges if they show a tendency to fray. Remove any tackings that may show on the right side of the cover and then turn up a ½in. (12mm) hem around the lower edges and tack in place. Clip out the excess fabric from the seam allowance at the corners of the top seam and press the seam up towards the top of the cover.

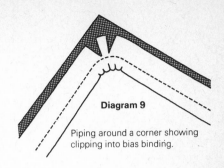

Diagram 9

Piping around a corner showing clipping into bias binding.

Place the cover on the cushion and pull the edges down over the edges of the calico and the wooden lid. Secure the four corners to the lid with gimp pins and then tack the cover to the lid all around using gimp pins spaced at about 1½in. (38mm) intervals. Stick a line of braid trimming around the lower edge of the lid to hide the gimp pin heads.

To cover the chest: Turn the chest over on to its back and paint a band of latex adhesive about 1½in. (38mm) wide along the lower edge of the front. Take one of the pieces of fabric cut to measurement A and press it to remove any creases, then place this on to the chest front so that the pattern, if there is one, is centred and the lower raw edge is level with the lower edge of the chest. Temporarily pin the centre of this edge in place with a gimp pin, then pull each side of the edge firmly but not too tightly outwards to the lower corners of the chest and press it down on to the adhesive. When the adhesive has dried, repeat the process with the top edge of the chest, taking care not to pull the fabric too tightly or it will distort. Remove the gimp pin from the centre of the lower edge. Do exactly the same with the back of the chest and then, when the adhesive has thoroughly dried, turn the chest on to one end. Allow about 1in. (25mm) of the ends of the back and front sections of fabric to extend over the end of the chest and trim the remainder away. Stick the overlaps in place on the end of the chest with latex adhesive. From the third piece of the fabric cut to measurement A, cut a section about 2in. (5cm) wider than the end of the chest, centring the design if there is one. Turn in a 1in. (25mm) hem down each side and stick this in place with latex adhesive. Place the fabric on to the end of the chest and stick the lower edge to the chest with latex adhesive. Tack the side edges in place with gimp pins spaced about 1½in. (38mm) apart, keeping the fabric taut but not too tightly pulled. Turn the chest up the other way and cover the opposite end in the same way. Turn the chest right way up, clip into the surplus fabric at the corners of the top edges wherever necessary for a smooth fit and then turn these edges to the inside of the chest and stick them in place with latex adhesive.

To make the lining: Cut a piece of calico 1in. (25mm) larger all around than the base of the chest, two pieces 1in. (25mm) larger all around than the front, and two pieces 1in. (25mm) larger than the ends of the chest. Join the back and front sections to the ends with $\frac{1}{2}$in. (12mm) seams and press the seams open. Join these sections to the base in the same way as the lining was made for the cushion top. Turn down a 1in. (25mm) hem around the open edge and baste it in place. Insert the lining into the chest and secure the top corners 1in. (25mm) below the top edge of the chest with gimp pins. Continue tacking gimp pins in place at $1\frac{1}{2}$in. (38mm) intervals around the top of the lining.

Replace the lid on to the chest and screw the hinges back on. Trim the lower edge of the chest with fringed braid so that it covers the raw edge of the fabric. Stick the braid in place with latex adhesive, used sparingly.

To cover the bolster: Measure the girth of the bolster and add on 1in. (25mm). Then measure the length and add on 1in. (25mm). Cut out a rectangle to this size from both calico and furnishing fabric. Measure the diameter of the bolster and add on 1in. (25mm). Then using a compass draw a circle of this size on to newspaper and cut it out to use as a pattern. Cut out two circles from calico and two from furnishing fabric. Join the two sides of the calico rectangle with a $\frac{1}{2}$in. (12mm) seam to make a tube shape and press the seam open. Stitch a calico circle into one end of the tube with a $\frac{1}{2}$in. (12mm) seam, easing the circle smoothly into the tube as you would insert a fitted sleeve into an armhole. Trim the seam to $\frac{1}{2}$in. (6mm) and then turn the lining right side out and insert the bolster into it. Turn in a $\frac{1}{2}$in. (12mm) hem around the open end of the tube and also around the other calico circle. Place the circle into the end of the tube and slipstitch in place.

Make up two lengths of piping and tack them to the right sides around the edges of the two fabric circles in the same way as described for the chest cushion. Machine stitch them in place using a piping foot. Make up the outer cover in exactly the same way as bolster lining and, when inserting the bolster, make sure that the seam allowances of the cover are turned towards the ends of the bolster rather than the sides to ensure a smooth finish. When the cover is completed the ends can be decorated with furnishing braid as shown in the photograph on p.28.

Buttoning and quilting using foam sheet

Some plain items of furniture can be greatly enhanced by the addition of matching buttons which sink down into their surface and give it a three-dimensional effect. Several ideas for using this type of decoration are given in this chapter, all of which are achieved by using polyether foam sheet over a firm base. Deep buttoning such as that seen on Chesterfield sofas and armchairs is quite a different technique to the kind of buttoning shown here. It is a complicated procedure of estimating the correct amount of fabric that is needed to make the pleats between the buttons, and then stuffing these sections so that they are all of uniform size and shape. Because it is so complicated I have not given any instructions for it here, but have used only the simpler, shallow buttoning.

Latex foam is not really suitable for buttoning because it can tear fairly easily and does not compress in quite the same manner as polyether foam. Successful shallow buttoning can be done with polyether foam and you can make some most attractive items. The best way of arranging the foam is to have a firm solid type on the base of the item and then a layer of softer foam on top of this. When the button threads are pulled taut the buttons will sink down into the top layer of foam but leave the lower one uncompressed. If the buttoning is purely decorative, for example on a bedhead, a soft layer of foam only is needed over perhaps a sheet of plywood or hardboard. The thickness of the soft foam used will depend on how deep you want the effect of the buttoning to be.

One of the main points to remember when tackling this type of decoration is to anchor all the buttons at the same depth, so that the foam is depressed the same amount under each one. If some of the buttons are noticeably deeper in the foam than others, the effect will be disappointing. Strong twine should be used to attach the buttons, and this should always be tied at the front of the work under the button, so that you can see how deep it sinks as you pull up the knot. Button moulds which you cover yourself can be obtained from haberdashery departments of large stores and these are quite suitable to use, particularly the type which is mainly plastic with a metal backing plate. Instructions for using them are supplied on their card, and they are made in a variety of sizes. If you prefer a more decorative effect you can use other kinds of buttons, but their choice will depend on the item you are buttoning.

Quilting: If you have a good strong sewing machine you can quilt a thin layer of foam in between a calico lining and the finished covering fabric, and this makes a most attractive outer cover for cushions, etc. You must use a large-sized machine needle, medium-thickness thread and a fairly large stitch. The best way to prepare for this type of job is to baste the foam and fabrics together along the lines you wish to stitch, then stitch along them with the sewing machine and remove the basting stitches afterwards. If you plan to tackle something like this, try it out first on a small offcut of foam and fabric to see if your machine will take the combined thickness. If the needle tends to jam in the work it may be because the thread is too thick for the size of needle, or because the needle is too fine for the fabric. Do not force the machine if it will not easily take the work or you may do it permanent damage. If the job is a fairly small one you can probably sew it by hand, using evenly spaced running stitches, and if you do sew it by hand you can use a thicker thread for a more dramatic effect.

Buttoned Cushion for a Chair

A shaped cushion makes a great deal of difference to the comfort of a wooden-seated chair. The one shown here is completely reversible and quite detatched from the chair itself so that it can be easily removed for cleaning. It is filled with polyether foam and so the whole cushion can be washed by hand without removing its cover. Coloured bias binding has been used to pipe the edges to match the colour of the fabric, and there are four fabric-covered, rustproof buttons on each side of the cushion which give interest to its plain surfaces.

To make this type of cushion you will need: A piece of 2in. (5cm) thick polyether foam at least as large as the chair seat; latex adhesive; enough calico to cover the foam cushion on both sides, plus extra all around for the seam allowance; the same amount of furnishing fabric; enough piping cord to go all around the edges of the cushion; the same amount of bias binding; sewing thread to match the colour of the fabric; eight large 'cover yourself' rustless button moulds.

METHOD

Make a newspaper pattern of the chair seat as shown in diagram 1. Place the paper on the seat and trim it to the shape and size of the front and back edges. Then shape the sides to allow for the upright supports of the arms and back if these are set into the seat. Fold the pattern in half down the centre as shown by the dotted line on the diagram and trim it carefully around the edges so that both sides are exactly the same size and shape. Open out the paper pattern and place it on to a piece of stiff card, mark around the pattern with a pencil, and then cut out the card $\frac{1}{2}$in. (12mm) larger all around than the paper. Make another card template exactly the same. Pierce a hole in the centre of each template and then place one on each side of the piece of foam and thread them tightly together through the pierced holes. Using a very sharp knife, cut through the foam around the edges of the card templates and then cut the thread and remove the templates. Spread a little latex adhesive on to the cut edges of the foam and leave it for a while until it becomes clear and tacky. Carefully pinch the edges together as shown in diagram 2 so that the adhesive sticks the top and bottom corners of the foam together to make a smoothly rounded edge all around the cushion.

Use one of your cardboard templates as a guide to mark two shapes on to the calico, and cut these out $\frac{1}{2}$in. (12mm) larger all around than the marked line. Cut out two similar shapes from the furnishing fabric. Join the calico shapes around the two sides and the front edge with a $\frac{1}{2}$in. (12mm) seam, leaving the back edge of the cover open. Trim the seam to $\frac{1}{4}$in. (6mm) wide all around and then clip into it around the

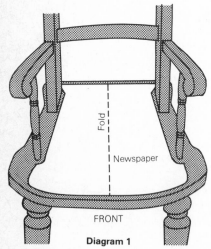

Diagram 1
Making a paper pattern of the chair seat.

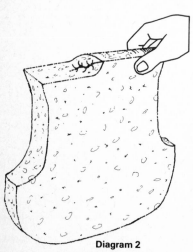

Diagram 2
Pinching the edges of the foam together.

curves for ease of turning as shown in diagram 3. Turn the lining right side out and insert the foam cushion into it, pushing it well into all the corners and shaped angles of the cover. Turn in a $\frac{1}{2}$in. (12mm) hem along the open back edge of the lining and slipstitch both sides of the cover together to close it completely.

Cut a length of piping cord long enough to go around all four sides of the cushion and then cut a corresponding length of bias binding. Open out the folds of the binding, place the cord in the centre of it and then re-fold the binding over the cord. Tack both layers of the binding together again, as close to the cord as possible to make a neatly covered piping cord. Pin and tack the piping around the right side of one of the fabric cut-out shapes, arranging it so that the line of tacking stitches comes $\frac{1}{2}$in. (12mm) from the raw edge of the fabric all around and the corded edge of the piping faces in towards the centre of the cushion. Place the joined ends of the piping at the back edge of the cushion. Machine stitch around the edges of the cushion cover to hold the piping firmly in place. Stitch as close to the cord as you can, using a piping foot on your sewing machine. With right sides facing, join the two furnishing fabric shapes together around the sides and front with a $\frac{1}{2}$in. (12mm) seam. Stitch as close to the piping cord as possible, sandwiching the bias binding between the two layers of fabric. Trim the seam to $\frac{1}{4}$in. (6mm) wide all around and then overcast it if the fabric is a type which frays easily. Clip into the curved parts of the seam allowance in the same way as for the calico lining and then turn the cover right side out and press it well all over. Turn in a $\frac{1}{2}$in. (12mm) hem down each side of the open back edge and tack this in place. Insert the cushion into the cover and slipstitch the back edge to close it.

Make up the covered buttons as described on the pack, using the cushion fabric if it is not too thick, or otherwise using a thinner matching or toning fabric. Thread a buttoning needle with doubled strong linen thread. Mark the four positions of the buttons to correspond on both sides of the cushion and then push the needle down into a mark on one side so that it emerges at the corresponding mark on the other side. Thread a button on to the needle and thread and then push the needle back through the cushion to the mark on the other side. Thread another button on to the thread and then draw up both ends of the thread and knot them very tightly as shown in diagrams 4 and 5, so that the buttons are drawn right down into the foam. Make these knots very secure and then trim off the surplus thread and tuck the cut ends under the button for neatness. Attach the other three pairs of buttons in the same way. If you like, you can attach lengths of tape or cord to the two back corners of the cushion so that it can be anchored to the chair by tying them either to the top of the legs or to the base of the back supports.

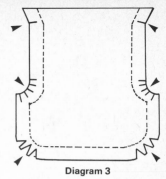

Diagram 3

Clipping into seam allowance.

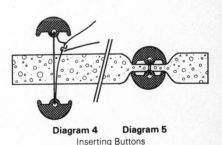

Diagram 4   **Diagram 5**

Inserting Buttons

A Toy Box with a Buttoned Seat

This useful large toy box can hold a whole wonderland of toys and keep the playroom looking really tidy as well as providing some extra seating. It is made from exactly the same type of blanket box as the ottoman shown on p.30, but this time only the lid has been covered with fabric. The front and sides have been painted and then decorated with a jolly chevron stripe in three contrasting colours. This was painted on using masking tape for the straight edges. No sewing is required for the top cushion. The fabric is simply stretched over a foam base and tacked to the sides of the lid with brightly coloured upholstery studs. Buttons have been added to the seat to give it extra firmness and also to look decorative, and these are anchored through the lid to leather washers on the inside.

To make a toy box like this you will need: A whitewood blanket box with a hinged lid; paint for the background colour plus three contrast colours; masking tape; a piece of 3in. (75mm) thick polyether foam the same size as the lid; a piece of thin, sheet foam $\frac{1}{2}$in. (12mm) larger all around than this; latex adhesive; calico for lining the cushion; upholstery fabric to tone with one of the paint colours; gimp pins; enamelled upholstery studs; six or eight large 'cover yourself' buttons; scraps of heavy leather to make the button washers; strong, thin twine.

METHOD

Remove the lid from the box by unscrewing the hinges. Replace the screws in their holes on the lid so that you can arrange the fabric around them and avoid getting bulky fabric edges under the hinges. Paint the front, sides and back of the box and the edges and inside of the lid with the main colour, giving it two or three coats if necessary to achieve a really smooth and even finish. When the paint has dried and hardened, mark out your chosen design and mask the edges of this with masking tape. Then paint in your contrast colours (this method of masking edges is only really suitable for designs consisting entirely of straight lines).

While the coloured stripes are drying you can cover the lid. Place this on the bench and plan the layout of the buttons as shown in diagram 6, keeping them equally spaced from each other and allowing a good margin all around the outside. When you are satisfied with your layout, mark it on to the lid in pencil and then drill holes carefully right down through the lid where each button will be, taking care to keep the drill at right angles to the surface of the lid. Smooth off any rough edges from around the holes with fine glasspaper. Place the thick piece of foam on to the top of the lid and secure it around the edges with latex adhesive. Place the thin sheet of foam on to this and secure it to the thick foam around the edges with latex adhesive, making sure that it overlaps the same amount all the way round.

Cut out a piece of calico to about 3in. (75mm) larger all around than the lid of the box and centre this on to the foam cushion. Secure it to the edges of the lid at each corner with a gimp pin to hold it temporarily

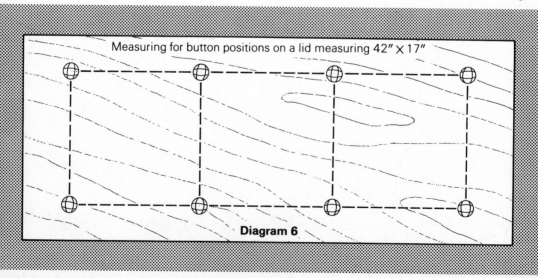

Measuring for button positions on a lid measuring 42" X 17"

Diagram 6

in place and then, working along the front of the lid first, compress the edge of the foam and tack the calico to the edge of the lid with gimp pins as shown in diagram 7. Do not hammer the tacks fully home, but leave them protruding a little in case you have to move them to adjust the tension of the calico later on. When the front edge is held in place in this way, do the same to the back edge and then to each end. At the corners fold the excess calico into two little pleats as shown in diagram 8, pull the fabric taut and insert the tacks as shown. Adjust the tension of the calico wherever necessary to obtain a smooth rounded cushion and then hammer all the tacks firmly home. Trim off the excess calico just below the line of tacks.

The main cover is put on in a similar way, except for a narrow single hem which is turned up around all four sides. The cover is tacked in place with upholstery studs instead of gimp pins, but gimp pins are used to hold it temporarily so that it can be adjusted before the studs are inserted. The finished lower edge of the fabric when it is attached extends to just below the edge of the calico, to cover the raw edges, and the excess fabric inside the corner pleats is trimmed away before finally securing. Space the studs about 2in. (5cm) apart around the front and sides of the lid and if you wish to economise use gimp pins along the back edge, since these will not show if the box is placed against a wall.

The buttons: For each button you will need a 1½in. (38mm) diameter circle of leather with a slit cut into either side as shown in diagram 9, and an 18in. (45cm) length of twine. Cover your buttons as directed on the pack, using offcuts from the main cushion fabric. Thread a buttoning needle on to one end of one of the lengths of twine and push the needle up through one of the holes in the lid and out through the top of the cushion. The twine should be pulled until it extends about 6in. (15cm) from the top of the cushion. Then remove the needle from the twine and thread it on to the other end. Push the needle again up through the hole and out through the cushion but do not pull the loop right through. Before you do this slip a leather washer on to the loop as shown in diagram 10 and then pull both ends of the twine level at the top of the cushion to draw the leather washer tightly to the underside of the lid. Leave the ends of twine hanging from the face of the cushion until all the button washers are in place. Position all the button threads and washers in the same way, making sure that both ends of each length of twine emerge from the cushion in the right place for each button. When all the threads are ready, slip a button on to one end of each and then draw up both ends of the twine and knot them securely behind the button head. Keep the tension of each thread the same so that all buttons will sink into the foam cushion to the same depth.

Place the lid on the box and screw the hinges in position. You can if you wish, slipstitch the corner pleats of the fabric for added neatness. This is best done on tweedy, heavily textured fabrics, but not really suitable on silky or fine ones where the stitches might show.

Buttoned Bedhead

If you have a divan type of bed, the head of which is placed against a plain wall you can make a bedhead like the one shown here and suspend it from a decorative curtain pole. There has recently been a revival of interest in the old-fashioned type of curtain pole, and it is now possible to buy these in a wide variety of styles and finishes. The one used here is a metal one with a white plastic coating and plastic wall brackets and

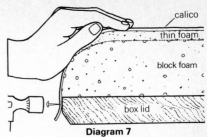

Diagram 7

Compressing the edge of the foam
to make a rounded cushion.

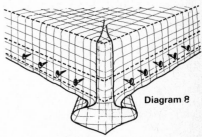

Diagram 8

Pleating calico over the corner
of the foam and tacking in place.

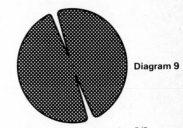

Diagram 9

Leather washer for buttoning S/S

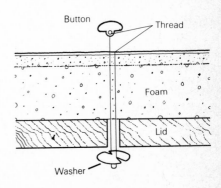

Diagram 10

finial ends. It is very easy to attach to the wall. The bedhead itself is very simple in construction. It consists of a sheet of plywood or hardboard, a sheet of foam and a piece of fabric. Both the foam and the fabric are stuck to the back of the board with adhesive so there is no sewing apart from attaching the buttons. The hanging loops are also made and attached with adhesive and so, provided you choose a good strong one, these will easily take the weight of the bedhead.

To make a bedhead like this one you will need: A curtain pole about 12in. (30cm) longer than the width of the bed; brackets and finials to match; a sheet of plywood or hardboard about 4in. (10cm) shorter than the width of the bed and about 2ft (60cm) wide; a sheet of $\frac{1}{2}$in. (12mm) thick foam about 2in. (5cm) larger all around than the board; calico; latex adhesive; a piece of fabric 3in. (75mm) larger all around than the board, plus extra for making the hanging loops and covering the buttons; some large button moulds; strong twine.

METHOD

Plan your button positions and mark these on to one side of the board, then drill them through using an electric drill or a brace and bit. The number of buttons you plan to use will depend on the width of the bed and how closely you decide to space them on the board. Cut or tear the calico into 3in. (75mm) strips and then stick these strips around the edges of the foam as shown in diagram 11, using latex adhesive and placing each strip so that it overlaps the edge of the foam by half its width. Place the foam, with the calico strips facing downwards, on to the table and leave it while the adhesive dries. Meanwhile trim off the corners of the board to a rounded shape and sand them smooth, then place the board in the centre of the foam and calico section. When you are sure that the adhesive holding the calico in place is quite dry, fold the edges of foam over the edges of the board and stick the calico to the edges of the board with adhesive, stretching the foam taut across the face of the board as you do so. Mitre the corners of the foam and trim them so that they lie flat on the back of the board. Place the rectangle of fabric, face down on the table and centre the padded board on to it. Then turn the edges of the fabric over on to the back of the board and stick them in place with adhesive. Stick both short ends first and then the two long sides. Pull the fabric taut across the face of the board and mitre the corners neatly at the back.

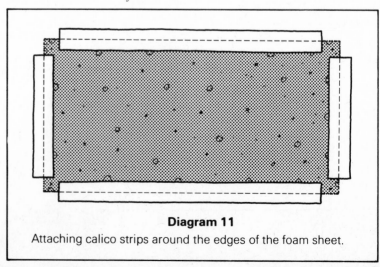

Diagram 11
Attaching calico strips around the edges of the foam sheet.

Decide how many loops you need to hang up the headboard and then cut out this number of strips of fabric each 12in. (30cm) by 8in. (20cm). Use a hot iron to press a single 1in. (25mm) hem down each long side of all these strips as shown in diagram 12 and then carefully stick these hems in place with latex adhesive. Fold each strip over as shown in diagram 13, so that there is 5in. (125mm) of one end extending below the other end. Stick the top end firmly in place, leaving enough of the folded part at the top free from adhesive to take the curtain pole. When all the loops have been made, arrange them along the top edge of the wrong side of the headboard as shown in diagram 14, so that the lower edge of each loop is 8in. (20cm) down from the top edge of the head-board. Stick them all firmly in place with latex adhesive. Cut out a num-ber of button washers from stiff leather (as described for the toy-box cushion on p.39, also cut off a 12in. (30cm) length of twine for each button and fold it in half. Slip the centre loop of each piece of twine on to a leather button washer and then thread a large needle with both ends of the twine. Push the needle down through one of the drilled holes in the board and out through the front of the fabric, unthread the needle and repeat with each of the other lengths of twine. When all of these are in place, turn the headboard over and attach a button at each of the thread positions. Draw up the twine and tie each button firmly in place, then trim off the surplus twine and push the cut ends under the buttons.

To attach the headboard to the wall: Stand it on the end of the bed and make a note of how high up the wall the tops of the loops come. Then screw the curtain pole brackets about 1in. (25mm) higher than this at each side of the bed, so that the headboard will hang free of the mattress. Thread the pole in through one of the brackets and then through the loops of the headboard and out through the other bracket. Tighten the holding screws on the brackets and attach the finial ends to the curtain pole.

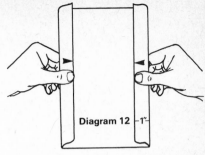

Diagram 12 ⊢1"⊣

Folding in hems at each side of hanging loop.

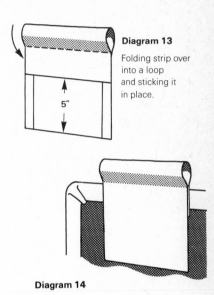

Diagram 13

Folding strip over into a loop and sticking it in place.

5"

Diagram 14

Attaching loop to back of headboard.

Chairs with webbing and padded seats

Not all seats have a solid base like the piano stool shown on p.14. Some chairs and stools have webbing holding the padding in place from below and the next two items show how to tackle the repair or replacement of broken or stretched webbing. When webbing is first put into a seat it is stretched very taut with the aid of a webbing stretcher or a block of wood as shown in picture 5 of the nursing chair instructions on p.55. This acts as a lever and enables you to get the webbing much tighter than you would be able to do if you just pulled it by hand. As the chair is used and the webbing gets older it tends to stretch and sag, and this often results in a hollow depression in the centre of the seat. It is not always necessary to remove the webbing completely to rectify this however. It is often possible to tighten it up simply by taking off one end of each length and re-tacking it to the frame in a tighter position. Care should be taken to place the tacks in slightly different positions the second time around so that they are not in the same holes as before, where they could work loose. If the webbing is at all torn or looks frayed and weak, it should be replaced with new webbing to ensure the safety of the seat. The padding may need a little extra added to it in order to obtain a good full shape and this can usually be done with kapok or wadding. If it is in really bad condition however, it can be completely replaced with a piece of latex or polyether foam which can be shaped into a curve around the edges by attaching it with strips of calico as explained in Chapter 3. Which ever way you pad the seat, try to get a smooth, slightly domed shape and make it just slightly higher than it needs to be since it will soon settle down with constant use.

Dining Chairs with Drop-in Seats

If you have never tackled upholstering before, this type of chair is ideal for a first attempt at re-newing seat webbing. The seat lifts right out of the chair frame and is very simple in construction, having a webbing base, a fibre or fibre and kapok filling and a one-piece fabric cover. When the seat looks rather hollow in the centre as the one shown does, it is usually because the padding has become compressed or the webbing has either broken away from the frame or been torn. In some cases the webbing will need to be replaced or renewed, and the padding re-distributed with perhaps a little extra added to it. In other cases all you will need to do is re-cover the seat with a new fabric, and this can sometimes be put on top of the old one, provided the seat does not fit too tightly into the chair. I am giving instructions below for the whole job of renewing webbing, padding and fabric. Then you can apply the relevant instructions to your own chairs.

To re-upholster this type of chair seat you will need: Calico for lining;

upholstery webbing (if the existing webbing is torn or weak); upholstery tacks; kapok for extra padding; gimp pins; upholstery fabric for the new cover; hessian or scrim for the underside of the seat.

METHOD

Remove the seat from the chair and check the frame for any loose joints, chips or bad scratches to the woodwork. Repair these defects with woodworking adhesive and wood filler. If necessary paint or varnish the frame as desired and whilst the paint or varnish is drying you can tackle the seat.

Place this, face down on a table or bench and remove from the back of its frame all the old tacks which are holding the cover in place as shown in diagram 1. If the seat has a webbing base it will probably have a separate cover on the base as well as the top of the seat, so remove the tacks holding this, carefully lift it off, and put it aside for later use. Turn the seat right way up and carefully lift off the cover by its edges, taking care not to disturb the padding more than you can help. Spread the cover out and iron it if necessary to make it lie really flat so that you can use it as a pattern. If it is really grubby, lay it on a piece of newspaper or brown paper, draw around it and cut out the shape. Then you can use either the old cover or this paper pattern as a guide for cutting out the calico lining. Also cut out an identical shape from the new fabric, making sure that the lengthwise grain runs from

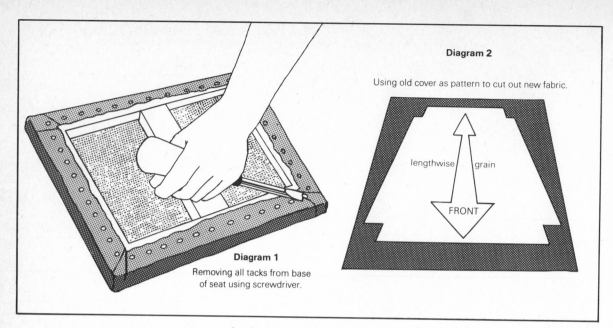

Diagram 2

Using old cover as pattern to cut out new fabric.

lengthwise   grain

FRONT

Diagram 1

Removing all tacks from base
of seat using screwdriver.

the front to back of the seat as shown by the arrow in diagram 2. If
you are using velvet for the new cover, the pile should run towards
the front of the seat to give good wear and correct shading. Carefully
lift off the padding and look at the webbing. If this is still strong and
taut, it can be left undisturbed, but if the tacks holding it have pulled
out of place or if the webbing has stretched and become slack, remove
the tacks, fill in the holes with wood filler and then replace the webbing
and tacks as shown in diagram 3. Place the tacks back into the frame
in slightly different places so that they are not in the same holes as
before. The webbing must be woven in and out alternately rather
like darning, as shown in the diagram, and should be really taut in
both directions. Where the webbing looks really weak and torn
replace it completely with new. An improvised webbing stretcher
can be made from a block of wood as shown in picture 5 of the nursing
chair instructions on p.55, so that you get it really taut. It is a good
idea to put a piece of hessian or calico over the webbing before replacing
the padding, to prevent little bits of padding from slipping out of the
bottom of the seat.

Replace the padding on to the webbing and examine it to see that
it is smoothly rounded in the centre. If there is still a slight flatness
or depression you will have to add some extra kapok to build it up
again. Do this by shredding the kapok into small pieces and building
it up gradually, as smoothly as possible. Arrange the calico lining over
the seat. Then turn the whole seat upside down and gently pull the
edges of the calico over on to the back of the seat frame. Tack the front
edge of the calico to the back of the frame with gimp pins and then do
the same with the back edge, making sure that the cover is drawn
evenly and fairly tightly over the padding. Mitre the corners of the
calico as shown in diagram 4 and then tack each side of the lining
firmly in place down the sides of the frame with gimp pins. Arrange
the new cover on to the seat, centring the pattern if there is one.
Tack the edges to the back of the frame in the same order as for the
calico lining and then trim off any surplus bulky raw edges of both
calico and fabric. Examine the hessian or scrim dust-cover for the base
if there is one, and if it is still in good condition re-fix it to the base of

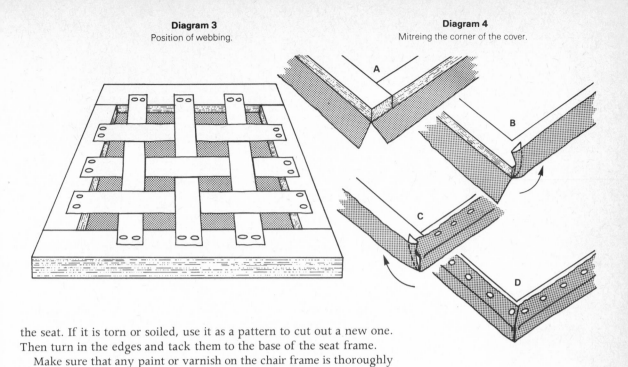

Diagram 3
Position of webbing.

Diagram 4
Mitreing the corner of the cover.

A

B

C

D

the seat. If it is torn or soiled, use it as a pattern to cut out a new one. Then turn in the edges and tack them to the base of the seat frame.

Make sure that any paint or varnish on the chair frame is thoroughly dry before inserting the seat, or you may find that the seat will stick in the frame and you will have difficulty in removing it for cleaning.

Chair with a Round Webbed Seat

Unlike the chair already described, the seat of this one does not lift out and so the webbing is slightly more difficult to get at in order to repair. The webbing base is covered by a horsehair padding with a layer of softer filling on top and the webbing is attached to the inside of the seat well. Care must be taken when attaching the webbing and the cover so as not to bruise the wood around the inner edge of the seat. A layer of hessian prevents the hair padding from falling out of the bottom of the seat and the top layer of kapok or wadding makes a smooth surface ready for the new cover. This type of chair often has a narrow lip around the top of the seat well, and when the cover is put on the tacks are placed within this lip. The fabric then sits just below the height of the wood surround and when the braid is put on it comes up to the same height as the top of the wood. On the chair we are using, however, the edge of the wood had been damaged at some time and so the braid trim was extended over the lip all around the seat to cover the chipped edge of the wood.

For a chair of this type you will need: new webbing; upholstery nails; new hessian if necessary; kapok and wadding; covering fabric; matching braid trim; gimp pins.

METHOD
First of all remove the old cover carefully and place it aside to use as a pattern later on. Lift out the padding and take off the hessian and examine the webbing. If this is slack or worn replace or renew it as already described for the dining chair. Cut out a new piece of hessian if necessary and arrange this over the webbing, or replace the old

piece if it is still in good condition. Place the padding back into the seat, re-shaping it if necessary and adding extra kapok or wadding to the top to get a good rounded shape. It is a good idea to cut a circle of wadding to fit exactly the shape and size of the seat well and to finish off with this so that the other padding will not move about when you are putting on the new cover.

Cut out the new fabric following the shape and size of the old cover, using it as a pattern. Place the cover on the seat, making sure that the design if there is one, is centred. If you are using a velvet, the pile should run from the back of the seat to the front. Attach the back edge of the cover first with gimp pins, taking great care not to strike the wooden moulding of the chair back with the hammer. When the back edge is secured, smooth the cover evenly over the seat and tack the front edge down. Then ease each side of the cover into shape and tack it in place on the frame with gimp pins. Trim off any excess fabric so that the edges of the cover fit neatly into the seat recess. Arrange the braid around the edge of the cover and either tack it in place with gimp pins, or stick it to the edge of the cover with latex adhesive.

Furniture
with webbing,
springs and padding

So far I have dealt with solid-based seats and those which have webbing holding the padding in place. Some dining chairs, however, and most old armchairs and sofas have springs between the webbing and padding to make the seat much deeper and more comfortable. These are usually single 'hour-glass' springs which are sewn to the webbing at their base and to a hessian cover at the top, which prevents the padding from slipping down between them. When this type of seat has sagged or become hollow in the centre many people think that it is because the springs have broken. This is very rarely the case. It is usually because the webbing holding them has broken and they have slipped out of position so that they are no longer supporting the padding properly. Very often a seat in this condition can be repaired without removing the padding and the cover. You can simply turn the chair upside down and renew or replace the webbing in the base, then sewing the springs back to this new webbing so that they are held in an upright position. If the webbing is not broken, but merely stretched and slack, new webbing can be tacked over it without removing the old. The springs should then be sewn to the new webbing. Sometimes, however, a chair is in such bad condition that you have to remove all the webbing, springs and padding and this is often the case where the frame needs some sort of repair. Since this is a fairly time-consuming procedure, and does make rather a lot of mess, it is as well to consider carefully before you buy a chair in really bad condition. If you do undertake to re-upholster it completely, then the results are well worth the time and energy spent on it as can be seen from the nursing chair before and after pictures on p.51 and p.57. With this particular chair I have shown photographs of all the different stages for dealing with its complete re-upholstery, and this basic procedure can be followed and adapted for most chairs constructed with webbing, hour-glass springs and padding. It is always advisable, however, to take note carefully of the construction of the furniture as you remove the padding, springs, etc., so that any differences in the way they are placed can be remembered when you put them all back.

Velvet Covered Dining Chair

These Edwardian dining chairs were discovered in an antique shop. They were covered in a grubby, faded and very torn patterned fabric and the stuffing was bulging out through the holes at the front corners of the seats. When the old fabric was taken off and the padding removed, the springs were found to be in good condition although the webbing holding them in place had rotted with age and needed replacing. Once this was done and the springs and padding had been replaced, the

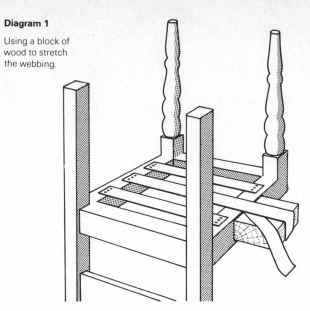

Diagram 1

Using a block of wood to stretch the webbing.

chairs looked a much better shape. They were given a calico lining underneath the main cover so that if the colour scheme of the dining room was changed at a later date it would be very easy to re-cover the chairs in a new fabric without disturbing the padding. The fabric chosen for the new outer cover was a practical Dralon velvet which is stain and crush resistant and greatly enhances the carved wooden frame.

To renovate this type of chair you will need the following materials: Upholstery tacks; new upholstery webbing; hessian or scrim; calico; twine for sewing in the springs; extra kapok for stuffing; gimp pins; upholstery fabric; latex adhesive; furnishing braid in a colour to match the new fabric.

METHOD

Carefully remove all the old tacks holding the cover in place and then lift it off and put it aside for making the pattern later on. Lift off the padding, in one piece if possible, and put this carefully on one side. Turn the chair upside down on the bench or table and remove all the tacks holding the webbing in place. Remove the webbing and springs, carefully examining them to see how each is positioned and sewn together. Pull out all the broken tacks and loose chips of wood from the frame and then fill all the tack holes with wood filler and leave to dry thoroughly. Replace all the old webbing with new upholstery webbing, stretching it taut across the frame with the aid of an offcut of wood as shown in diagram 1 (a photograph of this being done is shown on p.55. Weave the crosswise lengths of webbing in and out of the lengthwise ones as though you were darning. When all the webbing is in place turn the chair right way up, put back the springs and sew the base of each one to the webbing in their original positions. Cut a piece of hessian about 2in. (5cm) larger than the base of the chair, turn over a hem along each side and then tack this to the frame over the top of the springs, pulling it taut and tacking through the doubled thickness with upholstery tacks. When the hessian is firmly fixed in place, stitch the tops of the springs to it from above, so that they are held perfectly upright between the webbing and the hessian. (You will need a curved needle to do this.)

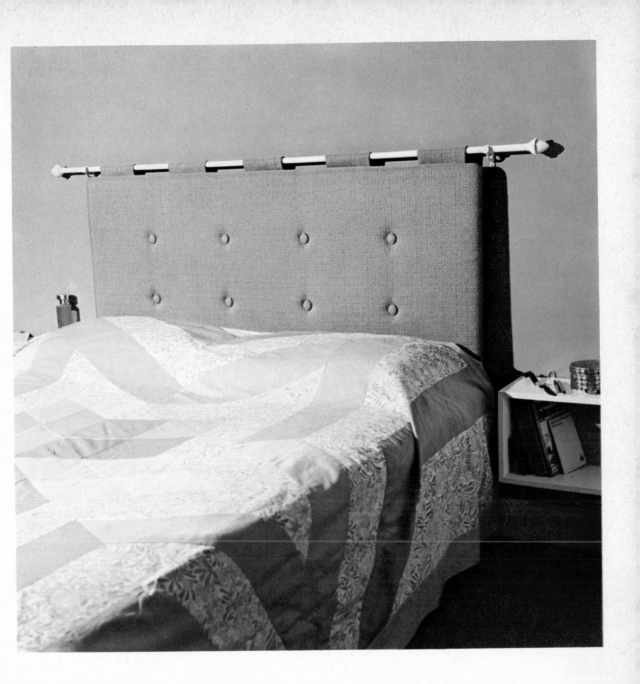

A buttoned bedhead (see page 39)

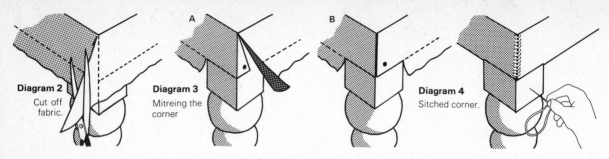

Diagram 2
Cut off
fabric.

Diagram 3
Mitreing the
corner

Diagram 4
Sitched corner.

Replace the padding on top of the hessian and add extra kapok if necessary to make it into a smooth full shape. Use the old cover as a pattern to cut out a lining from calico and place this on to the padding. Tack the lining temporarily in place along the back of the seat, placing one gimp pin in the centre and one at each side. Clip into the corners to allow for fitting around the upright supports of the chair back and then pull the lining smoothly down around the sides and front of the seat. On these particular chairs, the wood at the sides of the seat had been very badly treated and so the cover was extended right down over it, but on many chairs the wood will still be in good condition so the next step will depend on the state of the frame. The lining can either be tacked along the top edge of the side frame all around, or taken right down and tacked to the edges of the underside of the chair. In both cases, tack it temporarily in place all around first. Then after you have mitred the corners, you can adjust the cover to get rid of any wrinkles and then tack it permanently in place. If you are tacking it to the top of the seat the excess calico can be trimmed off close to the gimp pins holding it in place, but if you are attaching it to the underside the excess fabric can be left on since it will be covered later on with the hessian or scrim base lining. The method of mitring the corners is the same in both cases. Pull the excess fabric by the point of the corner and cut off most of the surplus as shown in diagram 2, then wrap the front edge of the calico around to the side of the chair and tack it in place with a gimp pin. Turn in a narrow hem at the corner of the side piece of calico and fold this over the front edge so that the fold of the hem comes right on the corner of the seat as shown in diagram 3. Tack this in place with a gimp pin and then thread a needle with strong thread and slipstitch the corner together to make a neat curved seam as shown in diagram 4. Once the corners are finished, the tacks all round the seat can be adjusted and hammered permanently home.

The main cover is put on in exactly the same way as the lining, and can extend to the top of the frame or the base as preferred. The corners should be stitched in the same way for a smooth outline. When the cover is finished, turn the chair upside down and cut a piece of hessian or scrim about 2in. (5cm) larger than the base. Turn over a hem on each side of this, then place it on the base of the chair over the webbing and tack it to the frame all around, pulling it taut in both directions.

To finish off the chair, cut a length of decorative braid to go around the sides and front of the lower edge, and another to fit across the back. Place these to cover the tacks along the edge if the fabric is joined to the top of the frame, or put it along the lower edge of the fabric if this has been turned over on to the base of the chair. This braid can either be tacked in place discreetly with matching colour gimp pins, or be stuck in place using the latex adhesive sparingly.

Edwardian Nursing Chair

At first sight this chair was a bit offputting I must admit. I found it
in a secondhand furniture shop and was attracted to it mainly because
the style of its carving, and the bobbins set into the back were very
similar in style to my dining chairs. I thought that, covered in the same
fabric, it would fit rather nicely into an empty space in the dining room.
On close examination it was found to have woodworm in the back
rail and in one back leg, but as this was not bad enough to have
weakened the frame I bought the chair and some woodworm killer
and set about completely renovating it. This turned out to be quite
straight-forward, but it did take quite a long time to complete. The
chair had been re-covered at some time over the top of the cover already
on it. Both these old covers were made from an imitation leather
material and had gone hard and brittle with age. Removing them in one
piece for the pattern was a bit difficult, but tears like these can always
be held together with sticky tape or safety pins to keep shapes accurate
for cutting out.

To completely renovate a chair like this you will need: New webbing,
(the amount needed can be estimated by measuring the old webbing)
upholstery tacks; strong twine for sewing in the springs and padding;
hessian; extra kapok if necessary to supplement the stuffing; wadding
in sheet form; fabric for the new cover; matching gimp pins; matching
or toning braid or gimp.

Dining chair with a drop-in seat (see page 42)

Dining chair with a round, webbed seat (see page 45)

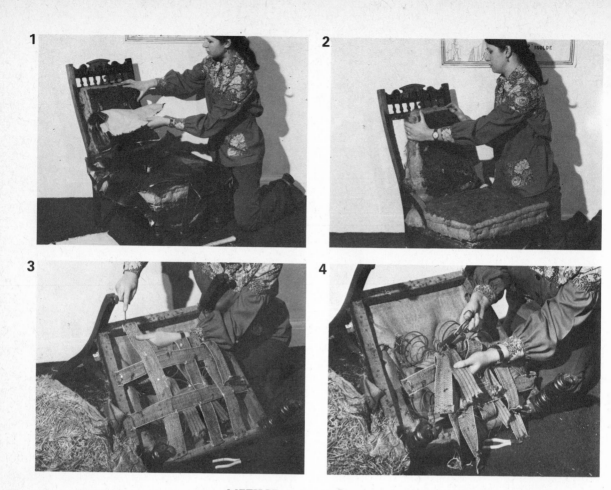

METHOD

Step 1. Prise out the studs or tacks holding the cover in place and try to remove this without tearing it too much. Label the sections of the old cover as you take them off and place them aside to use as patterns for the new cover later on.

Step 2. Pull out the tacks holding the padding to the frame and lift this off carefully from both the back and the seat. It is a good idea to wrap each section of padding carefully in a dust sheet or other old piece of fabric and place it out of the way since it does tend to leak a bit and can make rather a mess on the floor.

Step 3. Turn the chair upside down and remove all the tacks holding the webbing in place. You can see from the picture that this had been renewed at some time over the top of the existing webbing as described at the beginning of this chapter. You can also see here that the padding of the chair consisted mainly of wood wool, which meant that the chair was not too heavy and could be moved about very easily.

Step 4. Take an old pair of scissors and cut the twine which holds the springs to the webbing and the hessian. Take out the springs, brush them with a stiff brush to get rid of any dust and bits of padding and then place them carefully aside. Take out the tacks holding the hessian to the top of the seat frame, remove the hessian, and then go over the whole frame removing as many of the old nails and tacks as you can. Now that the frame is stripped down you can make any repairs which may be necessary. You can also tackle woodworm and strip and re-varnish the frame if desired.

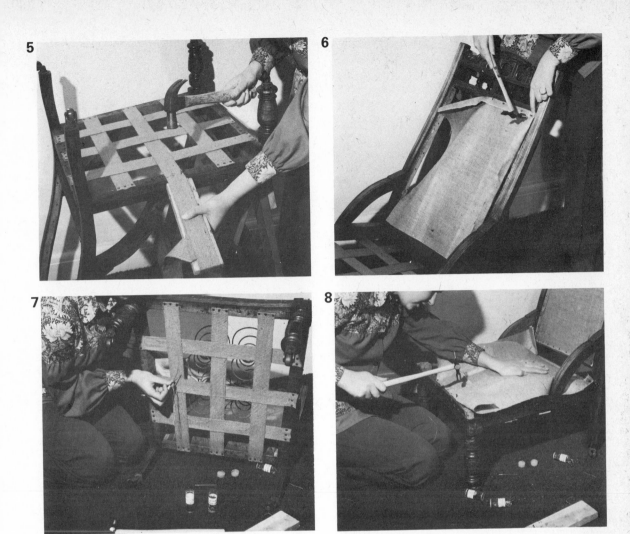

Step 5. Put the new webbing into the base of the seat using a block of wood as shown to stretch it really taut. Avoid placing tacks in the holes made by previous nails and tacks or they may work loose, try to get the webbing more or less in the same position as the original. You will find a trestle or an old saw horse very useful for balancing the chair seat so that you can get at the base more easily.

Step 6. Cut a piece of hessian about 3in. (75mm) larger all around than the inside of the back frame, turn over a hem all around this and tack it on to the frame with the hem turned out towards the front as shown. This makes a much stronger edge than if the hem were turned the other way.

Step 7. Place the springs, one at a time, into the base of the seat and sew each one to the top of the webbing with strong twine so that they will not be able to move about under the padding when the chair is being used.

Step 8. Turn the chair right way up again, cut a piece of hessian to cover the seat, plus a generous hem allowance all around. Tack the back edge of this in place and then pull it tightly to the front edge of the chair, compressing the springs firmly with one hand whilst you tack the front edge in place. Do the same with both the side edges, turning the hem of the hessian towards the top of the seat as shown.

55

Velvet-covered dining chair (see page 47)

Edwardian nursing chair (see page 51)

9

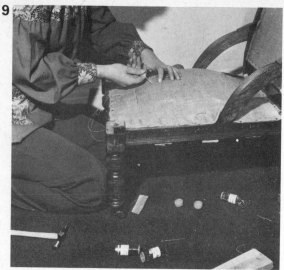

10

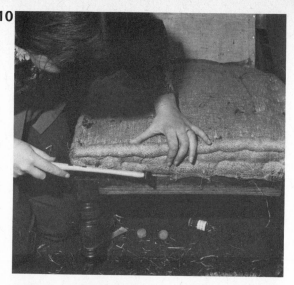

11

12

Step 9. Push each spring into an upright position underneath the hessian and when they are all correctly placed stitch them to the hessian with twine, using a curved needle to sew under the rim of the spring.

Step 10. Place the padding on to the seat and tack its lower edge to the top edges all around the frame. If the padding is leaking very badly you might like to wrap it in a piece of hessian just to keep it all in one piece. The hessian can be spread over the top of the padding and then tucked in underneath, just like making a bed. The lower edge of this new hessian can then be tacked to the top of the frame.

Step 11. Place the padding on to the back of the chair and tack it in place in the same way as for the seat padding. Then take a long needle and stitch the padding right through to the hessian chair backing with twine so that it will not slip down inside the cover when the chair is used.

Step 12. If the padding has become very flattened, build up the top with some extra kapok to make it smoothly rounded. Finish off by placing a sheet of wadding on to both the seat and the back cushions. Tuck the ends of this neatly down the back of the seat as shown.

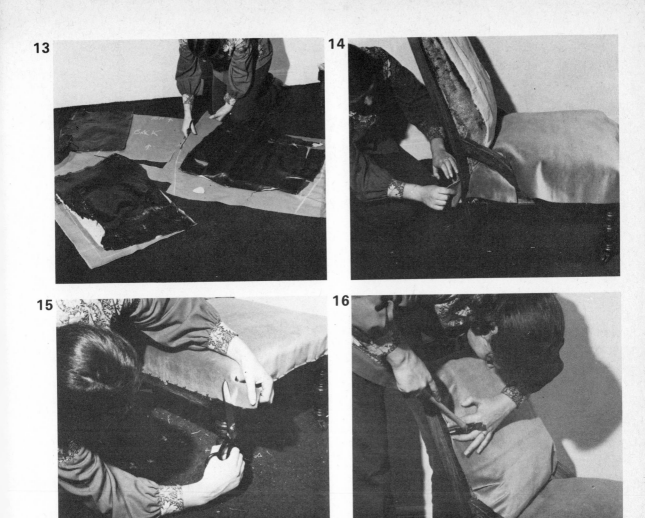

Step 13. Spread out the old cover and use it as a pattern for cutting out the new fabric. Mark the back of each new piece to identify it and, if you are using velvet or corduroy or a fabric with a one way design, mark this with arrows to get the direction right on all sections. The pile should run down the back of the chair and across the seat from the back to the front.

Step 14. Arrange the seat cover on to the chair, clipping into it wherever necessary to allow for the upright supports of the arms and back. Tuck the back edge firmly down the back of the seat and pull it out at the back as shown. Then adjust the cover so that it is correctly positioned on the seat.

Step 15. Tack the front and side edges of the cover temporarily in place and then work your way around the cover, adjusting the fit and tacking the side and front edges permanently in place. Trim some of the surplus fabric from the front corners as shown, leaving a narrow hem to turn in before sewing. Trim the front and side edges of the cover in a straight line all around.

Step 16. Place the back cover on to the chair and pull its lower edge down the back of the seat in the same way as for the seat cover. Tack the top and side edges temporarily in place and then adjust them to fit smoothly and tack them permanently in place all around.

Chaise longue (see page 65)

OPPOSITE *Armchair (see page 70)*

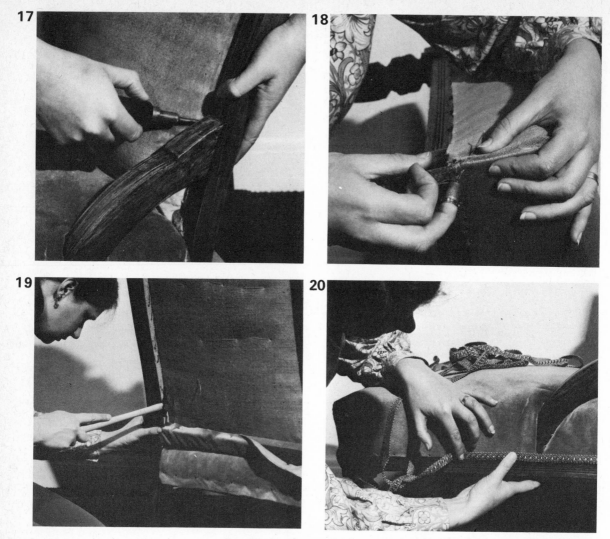

Step 17. In places which are very difficult to get at, such as behind the wooden arm supports, you can use a magnetic panel-pin punch to insert the gimp pins as shown here. This will help to prevent damage to the frame which could be caused if you attempt to use a hammer.

Step 18. Fold the edges of the front corners neatly into place as shown and slipstitch them together edge to edge with strong thread, using a large darning needle. Do the same with the top corners of the seat back cover.

Step 19. At the outside back of the chair pull the lower edge of the seat cover firmly down and tack it to the lower rail. Then pull the lower edge of the upright cover firmly and tack this to the rail above as shown. Trim off any surplus fabric from both edges and then place the outer back cover in position and tack it to the frame around the edges with gimp pins.

Step 20. Cut a length of braid to go around the sides and front of the lower edge of the seat and either tack this in place with gimp pins or stick it sparingly with latex adhesive. Cut another length and attach to the sides and top of the seat back, and a third length to cover all four edges of the outer seat back cover.

Chairs and sofas
with padded arms

Now that we have tackled chairs with sprung seats and padded backs we can go one stage further and look at some furniture which has padded arms. The arms will vary a great deal in shape and size of course, depending on the style of the furniture, but generally speaking they are all tackled more or less in the same way. Where the padding is in good condition it is not usually necessary to remove it, but this does have to be done on some of the more complicated shapes which are made up of two or more sections and where each section is covered separately. This is true of the chaise longue shown on p.65. The backrest here consists of a main cushion with a smaller scroll-shaped cushion on top and this top piece has to be removed in order to get at the top of the fabric which covers the main cushion.

Where the ends of arms are rounded or scroll shaped the covering fabric will have to be pleated in order to fit it smoothly around the front of the arm and this can be done in two ways. You can start with a box pleat in the centre top of the arm, and then fit the other pleats into this from both sides until the fullness is taken up as shown in diagram 1. The other way to tackle this is to make all the pleats running in the same direction as shown in diagram 2. If you are using this second method you must remember to reverse the direction of the pleats on the opposite arm so that they all run outwards, or they all run inwards on both arms. This type of pleated arm end usually terminates either with a wooden centre panel trimmed around the edges with braid, or with a fabric panel trimmed in the same way. Where there is a fabric panel it is often padded to make it stand out in the centre before being trimmed with braid.

The general instructions for the armchair shown on p.61 can be adapted for use with a sofa, the main difference being in the added length of the back and the seat. The arms will be more or less the same. In order to make a wide enough piece of fabric for covering the seat and the back sections of a sofa it is necessary to seam several pieces together and this is done in the following way: One main piece of fabric is used for the centre of the back and then extra is added to each side, matching up the pattern wherever necessary. The same method is used for piecing the seat cover together. If you are using expensive fabric and wish to economise, the area which extends out of sight down the back of the seat on both the back cover and the seat cover can be substituted with a piece of hessian or strong calico. These added sections are called flies. The same thing can be done with the part of the arm cover which fits unseen down the side of the seat. If your armchair has a loose box cushion in the seat, the fly can be extended out over the main part of the seat to within about 6in. (15cm) of its front edge. Then the cushion will cover this when it is in position. The cushion itself can have a calico cover on the underside, unless you need it to be

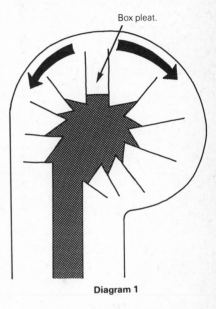

Box pleat.

Diagram 1

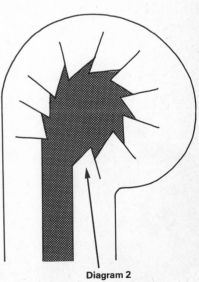

Diagram 2
Pleats all going in the same direction.

Small button-backed chair (see page 74)

reversible to even out the wear. Some sofas have arms which are hinged so that they can be dropped down in order to make the sofa into a bed. In this case it is much easier to unscrew the hinges and remove the arms before recovering, so that you will not have to wrestle with the whole sofa whilst you are doing this.

Chaise Longue

A chaise longue which has been properly re-upholstered would cost you quite a lot of money in an antique shop, but occasionally you do come across one which has not been renovated and this will, of course, be a great deal cheaper to buy. There is a lot of work in an item of this size and re-upholstery should not be undertaken lightly, but if you do decide to tackle the job yourself the results are well worth it, as you can see from the colour photograph (p.60). The condition of the one shown here was not too bad to start with. The webbing was absolutely rotten and the springs had gone right through it, but the padding was still in good shape and none of it was missing. One of the castors had broken off and the chaise rocked about on its legs, so all the castors were removed to be replaced with new ones later on. There was no woodworm present in the frame but the varnish was a bit scratched and rather the worse for wear and so I went over it with button polish whilst the frame was stripped down. If the wood had been a better quality I would have stripped off the old varnish and completely re-polished it, but on close examination it proved to have no interesting grain to enhance in this way. A chaise longue of the shape and size shown here will take about four yards of 48in. wide furnishing fabric, allowing for the one-way design. Try and match up the pattern on the seat, the back cushion and the scroll end if you can, and if you are using a velvet the pile should run from the scroll end down to the foot.

To re-upholster a chaise longue you will need the following materials: Webbing for the base (I used about 14 yards for this one but you can estimate how much you will need by measuring the existing webbing); large upholstery tacks; gimp pins; calico for lining; extra padding if necessary; cotton or synthetic wadding; hessian; furnishing fabric for re-covering; matching furnishing braid or gimp.

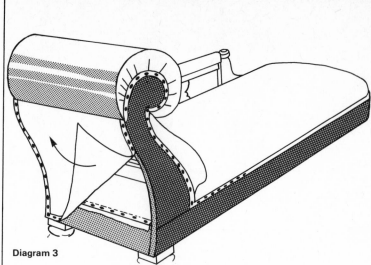

Diagram 3

Remove outer back cover to expose edges of main cover and cushion covers.

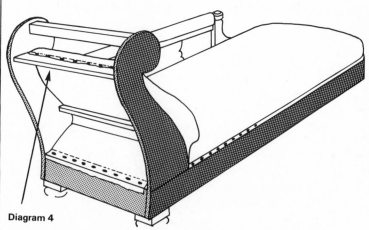

Diagram 4

Remove scroll padding from top of backrest.

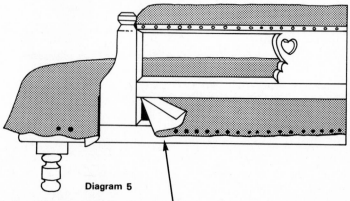

Diagram 5

Tucking calico lining down around arm support and tacking it in place.

METHOD

Remove the cover from the outside of the backrest so that you can clearly see the rails holding the wooden parts of the back in place and the edges of the fabric which is tacked to them as shown in diagram 3. Place this cover carefully aside to use as a pattern for cutting out the new cover later on. Prise out all the tacks holding the top scroll cushion cover and cushion in place and carefully remove them both from the top of the backrest. Treat the cushion with great care as it is likely to be full of loose woodshavings which need to be retained for putting back later on. Try to keep this section of padding as near as possible to its original shape. You will now be able to see clearly how the main cushion of the backrest is held in place on the rails as shown in diagram 4. Remove all the old tacks holding this in place and put it carefully aside for use later on. Remove all the old tacks from the frame of the backrest. Take out the tacks holding the main seat cushion cover and cushion in place. Remove the cover and then the padding, keeping it all in one piece if you can so that it will be easy to put back again.

Take off the hessian from the top of the springs, the springs themselves, and the webbing from below them. Separate the springs from the hessian and webbing, which can be discarded. Pull out all the old tacks from the frame. Then fill in any large holes, make any repairs which may be necessary and then clean the frame, sand it down and re-polish if necessary. You will now have a bare frame apart from the padded arm. This is the best time to replace the castors if they are broken or do not work properly. Whilst the frame is upside down, replace the webbing with new, stretching it tightly with the aid of a block of wood as shown in the instructions for the nursing chair on p.55. The webbing should be arranged as shown in the photograph, so that each spring sits on the doubled part where it crosses over another section. An extra length of webbing is threaded from front to back between each line of springs for added strength. The lengthwise pieces of webbing are secured to the centre stretcher of the frame with a doubled piece of webbing, which is folded in half lengthwise and tacked in place over them. When all the webbing is firmly in position, replace the springs one by one and sew each one firmly to the webbing with twine.

Turn the frame right way up and cut a piece of hessian to fit over the top of the springs, allowing a generous turning all around. Tack this in place to the top of the frame, pushing the springs down as flat as you can whilst you fix the hessian in position. Make sure that all the springs are perfectly upright between the webbing and the hessian and then sew the top of each one firmly to the hessian with twine, using a curved needle. Carefully replace the padding on top of the springs and arrange it as flat as possible. Add extra kapok to fill any shallow dents and to give it a good shape around the edges, then cover the whole padding with a piece of wadding cut to the size of the top of the seat.

Cut out a piece of calico a little larger than the old fabric cover and arrange it over the seat, clipping into it where the arm support breaks into the line of the seat and turning in the surplus calico before tacking it in place as shown in diagram 5. Tack the calico in place along the back of the chaise longue first as shown in diagram 5, and then pull it taut across the padding and tack it temporarily in place along the front edge. Now pull the calico at the foot of the chaise and tack it temporarily in place here. Then pull it at the top end and tack this temporarily in place (Diag. 6). Return to the foot end, gather the calico into little pleats at the two corners as shown in diagram 7 and tack these

How the webbing is positioned with the springs supported on each cross-over section

67

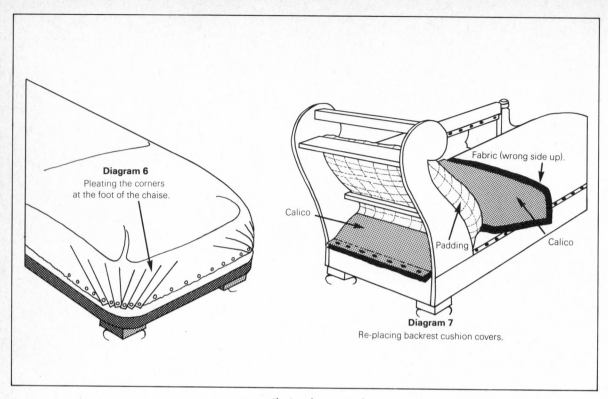

Diagram 6
Pleating the corners
at the foot of the chaise.

Fabric (wrong side up).

Calico

Padding

Calico

Diagram 7
Re-placing backrest cushion covers.

temporarily in place. Work your way around all four sides of the seat, adjusting the tension of the calico and tacking it permanently in place with gimp pins. Then trim off the surplus fabric close to the tacks. Cut out the main fabric cover using the old cover as a pattern and attach it to all four sides of the seat in the same way as for the calico, trimming the edges neatly in line all around so that the braid will easily cover them.

Remove the tacks holding the arm cover in place and take this off and use it as a pattern for cutting the new cover. Adjust the stuffing of the arm if necessary, adding extra kapok to fill in any dents or hollows. Next place the new cover on to it and tack it in place all around with gimp pins, pulling the fabric taut over the padding to give a smooth finish. Trim off the edges of the fabric around the arm and attach a length of braid over the raw edges to cover them. This can be stuck on with latex adhesive, tacked in place with gimp pins in a matching colour, or you can use decorative domed upholstery studs.

Replace the main backrest on to the frame and tack it in place. Add extra padding if necessary and cut a piece of wadding to fit over the cushion to give it a smooth outline. Use the old cushion cover as a pattern to cut out a calico lining, making this a little larger all around than the old cover so that you have something to hold on to whilst you pull it into position. Also cut out this shape from furnishing fabric, matching the pattern to the top section of the seat cover if you can. Place the furnishing fabric and calico together at the lower edges. Then, treating them both as one fabric, tuck this lower edge down the back of the seat as shown in diagram 8, keeping the calico layer on top and the fabric underneath, with its right side facing towards the seat of the chaise. Tack both the calico and fabric in place along the lower back rail as shown in diagram 8. Lift up the top edge of the

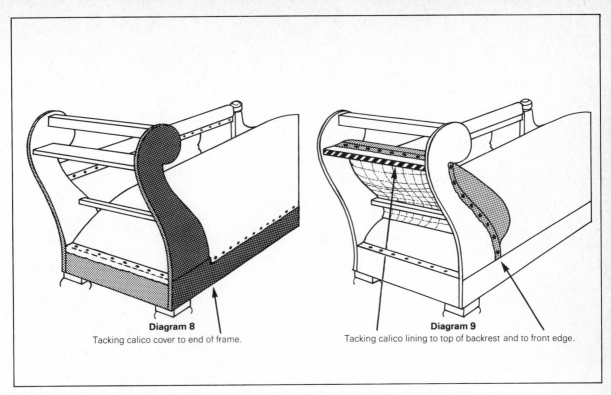

Diagram 8
Tacking calico cover to end of frame.

Diagram 9
Tacking calico lining to top of backrest and to front edge.

calico lining, pull this up over the cushion and tack it along the rail at the top of the padding as shown in diagram 9. Pull the calico tightly and evenly up over the padding so that there are no bumps and bulges. Then, when the top is secured, tack the front and back edges of the calico in place as shown in diagram 9, fitting the back edge carefully around the end of the arm where it joins the wooden upright section. When the calico is secured all round, trim off any surplus fabric from the edges and then secure the outer cover in the same way, trimming off the edges of this in a neat line ready for the braid trim.

The top scroll-shaped cushion is put on and covered in exactly the same way as this. The lower edge of calico and fabric are both secured to the same rail as the top of the backrest cushion. Then, when they are pulled up over the cushion, they are tacked to the underneath of the other side of this rail, which is shown shaded dark in diagram 9. The front and back side edges of both the calico and cover will have to be pleated around the curve of the scroll in neat and even pleats as you can see from the colour photograph (p.60).

The final stages are to replace the back outside cover as shown in diagram 3, tacking the top edge of this to the underside of the shaded rail in diagram 9, and the sides and base to the main parts of the frame. A specially-shaped panel must be made for the back end of the upright, to cover the raw edges of the cover, and this can be cut out following the shape of this section of the old cover. When all sections of cover are in place, the raw edges everywhere are trimmed with braid or gimp in the same way as the arm.

NOTE: These instructions refer specifically to the type of chaise longue in this book. You may find that the chaise you plan to re-upholster is differently shaped. The basic procedures are the same, however, and you should have no difficulty in adapting these instructions. The

main thing to bear in mind is to observe how the old cover is attached and it is well worth making a few rough sketches as you remove it, especially if you will be working on it over a long period of time and may forget minor details.

Armchair

This is a fairly typical old armchair, a little old-fashioned perhaps, but nevertheless extremely confortable to sit in and very hard wearing. The cover for it had been made up from two different types of green velvet, one plain and one patterned and these had been seamed together in such a way that the pattern occurred in the centre of the back, seat and arms. Unfortunately the plain velvet was a different kind from the patterned and had faded to quite a contrasting colour which gave the chair a very odd look indeed. Apart from this the chair itself was in fairly good condition and did not need re-webbing or springing. When the old cover was removed it was found that the back of the chair was sprung as well as the seat, but this back section had a pre-fabricated sprung unit instead of the individual type of

70

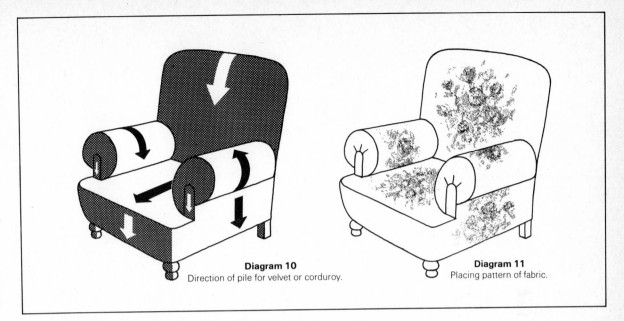

Diagram 10
Direction of pile for velvet or corduroy.

Diagram 11
Placing pattern of fabric.

springing found in the seat. This unit was held in place by webbing in the usual way as can be seen from the photograph (p.71). Since the webbing, springs and padding of the chair were in such good condition all that was needed was a new cover and for this I chose a tweed-look synthetic fabric. A chair like this will take about five yards of 48in. wide furnishing fabric, unless you are using a patterned one with a large repeat, in which case you must allow extra for matching up the pattern. The direction of the pile of velvet or corduroy should run in the direction of the arrows shown in diagram 10, and if the fabric is patterned the main design should occur in the centre of the back, seat, arms and outside panels as shown in diagram 11. The method of attaching the new cover is basically the same as for the nursing chair and the chaise longue; only the shapes are different.

For a chair of this type you will need: about five yards of 48in. wide furnishing fabric; gimp pins; new webbing and tacks if necessary; extra padding and wadding if necessary; hessian for the base if necessary; braid or gimp trimming; decorative domed upholstery studs.

METHOD

Turn the chair upside down, remove the hessian from the base and check to see that the springs and webbing are in good condition. If not, remove the webbing and replace it with new as described for the chaise longue on p.67, stretching the webbing taut with a block of wood as described. Sew the springs to the webbing in their original positions with twine. Whilst the chair is upside down, check the castors to see that they revolve freely and are quite firmly attached to the legs, if not, make any repairs or replacements which may be necessary. Turn the chair right way up again and remove outer covers from the back and arms of the chair so that the side and back rails are exposed. Examine these rails to see exactly how the old cover is attached and make a note of this. Carefully remove all the tacks holding the various sections of the cover in position, then lift the sections carefully off the chair. Press the pieces of the old cover out flat and use them as a pattern for cutting out the new fabric, remembering to match up patterns wherever possible and check the direction of the pile if there is one.

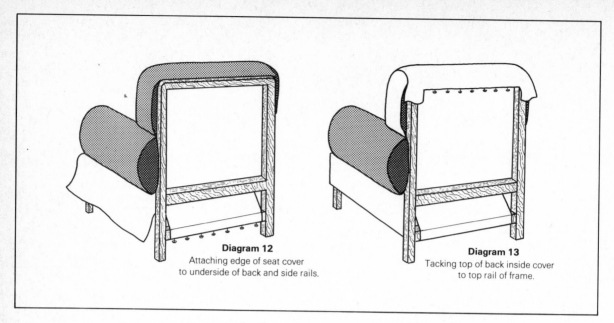

Diagram 12
Attaching edge of seat cover
to underside of back and side rails.

Diagram 13
Tacking top of back inside cover
to top rail of frame.

Make the new cover slightly larger all around than the old one. You may find that the chair has a calico cover under the old top one but if this is not so you may like to make one yourself before putting on the new fabric. This is not strictly necessary, but it does help to hold the padding firmly in place and makes it easier to re-cover the chair at any time without disturbing the stuffing. If you decide to make a lining, cut this out exactly as for the main cover, making it a little larger all around so that you have plenty of fabric to pull on at the edges to get it really smooth and taut. The method of attaching the lining and the main cover are exactly the same and are as follows.

Starting with the seat of the chair, fill in any dents or hollows there may be in the padding with kapok and, if the seat is really lumpy, cut out a piece of wadding to fit right over its top surface. Place the wadding on the seat and then put the cover over it and tuck the side and back edges down around the sides and back of the seat and pull them out just above the lower rails of the chair. Clip into the corners of the cover wherever necessary to obtain a good smooth fit. Pull the back edge of the cover firmly over the back rail and then tack it to the underside of the rail as shown in diagram 12. Do the same with the two sides and then smooth the cover down towards the front of the seat. Pull it taut and temporarily tack it in place along the lower front rail. Mitre the front corners in the same way as for the nursing chair and then adjust the cover along the front edge and permanently tack it to the underside of the front rail. Sew in the front corners of the cover in the same way as for the nursing chair.

Cover the inside back of the chair next. Lay the cover over this, pull the top edge up and over the top of the chair back and tack it in place along the underside of the top rail as shown in diagram 13, clipping into the edge at each side to allow for the upright frame of the chair as shown in the diagram. Pull the base of this cover down to the rail which is just above the bottom rail, bring the fabric out under this rail and turn it up around the outside of the rail. Tack it temporarily in place. Now take each side of the fabric in turn, fold it around the back of the chair and tack it temporarily in place to the upright of the frame, pulling it evenly and smoothly around the padding.

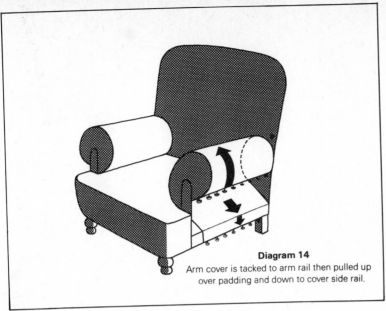

Diagram 14
Arm cover is tacked to arm rail then pulled up
over padding and down to cover side rail.

Go down each side of the cover, adjusting its fit, and when you are satisfied that it is quite smooth, hammer the tacks permanently in place. Do the same along the lower edge.

Place the arm covers in position on the arm padding. Tack the top edge of each to the underside of the top arm rail. Then pull the fabric up over the padding, down the inside of the arm, down the side of the seat and out at the lower rail as for the seat cover. Tack the lower edge in place in the same way as for the seat cover. (Diagram 14.).

(NOTE: On some chairs there may be a rail midway between the arm rail and the lower side rail of the chair and in this case tack the lower edge of the arm cover to the underside of this one instead of the lower rail.) Pull the back edges of the arm cover neatly around the back end of the arm padding, clip into them wherever necessary for a smooth fit, and then tack them securely to the frame. At the front of the arm, arrange the edge of the cover into neat little pleats all radiating from the centre and tack these to the front wooden part of the arm in the same way as shown on the scroll end of the chaise longue.

On the outside of the arm tack the top of the outer cover to the underside of the arm rail. Then pull the cover firmly down to the base of the chair and tack it to the underside of the lower rail so that it completely covers in the side of the chair. Neaten the front edge of this cover by tacking it to the upright part of the arm support and then neaten the back edge by folding it around the back upright and tacking it in place to the back of the frame. When both outer arm covers are in place attach the back outer cover in the same way, but instead of folding it around the corners of the back upright, turn in a narrow hem at each side and tack these in line down the extreme edges of the back of the frame. Cut out the two scroll-shaped panels for the front of the arms (from main fabric only) and tack these in place. Then trim around the edges of them with braid or gimp and upholstery studs. If you wish you can also trim around the lower side and front edges of the chair.

Cut a piece of hessian to fit the base of the chair plus an allowance for a hem all around. Fold this hem in place and then tack the hessian firmly to the base of the chair.

Making a pattern
when no old cover
is available

Occasionally you will come across a chair which has been stripped of its old cover, or where the old cover is worn and in such bad condition that you cannot use it as a guide or pattern for cutting out the new fabric. When this is the case, you will have to make a pattern first of all out of some other material, and then use this to estimate the amount of new fabric you will need to buy. I find that an old sheet is ideal for this, or you could use a pair of very old, faded curtains or any other large piece of fabric. The most important thing to remember when making a pattern like this is to allow generous hem and seam amounts wherever they occur, and to bear in mind that the rather flimsy fabric of an old sheet will tend to stretch around awkward corners very easily, whereas the new covering fabric may not, so it is best to allow extra for this when cutting out the shape.

Once you have draped the sheet on to the chair and trimmed away the surplus from the edges, always remove the pattern and fold it in half down the centre. Then you can make both sides of it exactly the same size and shape to avoid distortion. This is particularly important if you are planning to cover the chair in a patterned fabric, since a lop-sided design would be particularly noticeable. In order to be able to fold it accurately down the centre, always chalk or pencil a line on to the pattern fabric, down the centre of the chair back, the centre of the seat and the centre of the outer back cover, and then pin the top and bottom ends of these lines in position first. You can then work outwards from the top and bottom of each line, pinning the fabric as you go and making sure it is running smoothly over the surface of the chair. Patterns for arms are made in the same way as this and should be marked left and right on the pattern so that you cut them the right way out from the fabric. Also mark the front and back ends of the arms clearly on the pattern. Label all pattern pieces clearly and mark the top edge of each so that you have no difficulty in planning the cutting layout of the fabric to get the grain or pattern running in the right direction.

Small Button-backed Chair

When this chair was obtained it had already been lined in calico, but as there was no old cover to use as a pattern a new pattern had to be made out of an old sheet. This can be rather a tricky job to do since it must be really accurate or the new cover will not fit the chair properly. I am giving the instructions for this with step-by-step photographs so that you can see clearly the different stages of making the pattern and then attaching the new cover. The first thing you must do is to remove the hessian covering from the base of the seat and then loosen the bot-

tom edge of the outside back lining from the lower rail of the frame. When you have done this, you should be able to push your hand down the back of the seat and out just above the lower rail. It is important that the lower rail and the rail just above this are easily accessible, since this is where the lower edge of the inside back cover and the back edge of the seat cover are attached to the frame. The other preparation is to remove the buttons if there are any and place them aside for re-covering.

To cover a chair like this you will need: An old sheet to use as a pattern; dressmaking pins; loose cover pins; new fabric; gimp pins; sewing thread to match the fabric; braid or gimp to match the fabric; latex adhesive.

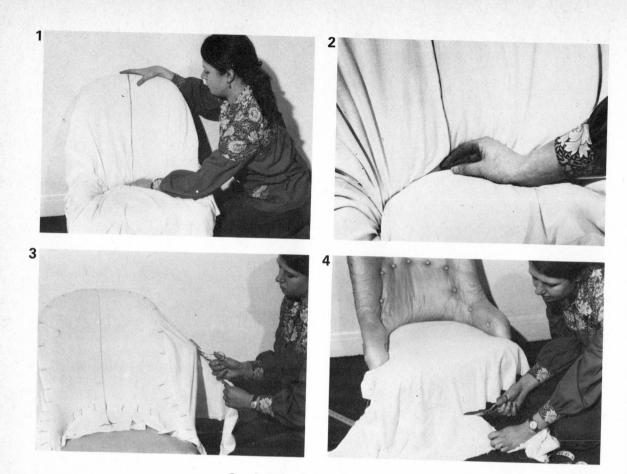

Step 1. Once the hessian has been removed and the back rails exposed as described above, place the sheet on to the inside back of the chair with a chalked or pencilled line running down the centre as shown. Make sure that enough sheet overhangs the top edge to make a decent hem. Then pin the sheet in place to the chair at the top and bottom of the drawn line, using either dressmakers pins or loose cover pins, whichever you prefer.

Step 2. Push the sheet down the back of the seat until you can feel it at the back lower rail. Make sure it is smoothly fitting down the centre back of the chair and then mark the centre of the sheet where it touches the back rail. Lift the sheet off the chair and find the mark you have just made. Then cut or tear across the sheet about 3in. (75mm) below this mark.

Step 3. Place the pattern back on the chair and attach it around the top and bottom inside edges with pins as shown. When you are satisfied that it is smoothly fitted all over the front, trim away the edges of the sheet to within about 3in. (75mm) of the top and side edges. Remove the pattern from the chair, fold it in half down the centre line, and trim both sides to the same shape around the sides and top.

Step 4. Take another piece of sheet and place it on to the chair seat, pushing it down the back of the seat and out at the lower rail as for the first pattern. When it is smoothly arranged on the seat, trim off the surplus fabric around the front edge to within about 2in. (5cm) of the lower edge of the front rail as shown. Remove the pattern from the chair, fold it in half down the centre, and trim both sides level as already described.

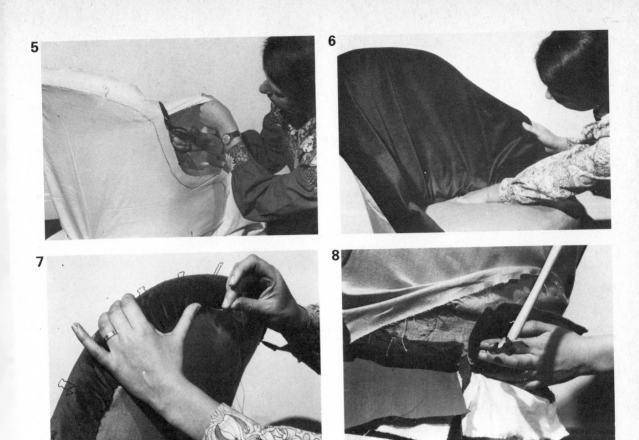

Step 5. Place another piece of sheet on to the outside back of the chair with a marked line down the centre back. Pull it smoothly around the outside of the chair, pinning it in place around the top and bottom edges. Then trim off the excess sheet to within about 2in. (5cm) of the top seam line. Remove the pattern from the chair, fold it down the centre line, and trim both sides to the same shape.

You are now ready to cut out the new fabric, taking care to keep the drawn centre lines running along the lengthwise grain, and making sure that the design or pile of the fabric is the right way up.

Step 6. Arrange the inside back cover on the chair and secure the centre of the top edge to the chair with a loose cover pin. Clip into the lower edge wherever necessary to allow for a smooth fitting around the curve of the seat back, and then tuck the lower edge down the back of the seat and pull it out at the back rail.

Step 7. Smooth the top edge of the cover around the top of the chair, pinning it in place at intervals with loose cover pins. Clip into the seam allowance around the sides and the top where necessary to allow it to fit smoothly and then attach this top seam allowance to the top edge of the chair around the outside back. If the chair has a wooden frame here, the cover should be tacked in place with gimp pins. If not, it can be sewn to the lining using a curved needle as shown. Trim off the excess seam allowance.

Step 8. Pull the lower edge of the back cover firmly and smoothly down the back of the seat and then turn it up around the top back rail as shown and tack it in place with gimp pins. You may find that you have to make a small pleat in the front of the cover where the arm meets the upright part of the frame in order to take care of the fullness around the curve.

9

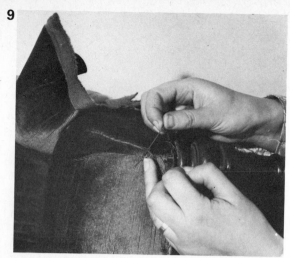

10

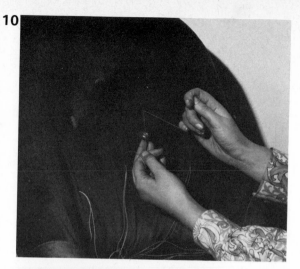

11

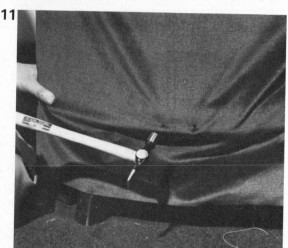

12

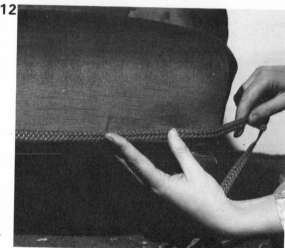

Step 9. Place the seat cover on the chair and tack it in place around the lower front and side edges. Clip into it at the front of the arms and push the side and back edges down around the sides and back of the seat and out at the back rail. Pull these edges firmly so that the cover fits smoothly over the seat and then tack them to the underside of the rail with gimp pins. Mitre the front corners of the cover and stitch them.

Step 10. Cover the buttons in matching fabric and make leather washers for them as described in the toybox instructions on p.39. Thread a buttoning needle with strong twine and attach all the buttons to the back of the chair in the desired positions, pulling the thread evenly so that they all sink down to the same depth.

Step 11. Place the outside back cover on to the chair and either tack or stitch the top edge in place. Pull the lower edge smoothly around the sides and back of the chair and tack it to the underside of the lower rail with gimp pins.

Step 12. Cut a length of matching braid or gimp to go around the outside top and back edges of the chair and attach it either with matching gimp pins or with latex adhesive. Cut another length to go around the entire lower edge of the chair and attach this in the same way.

To finish off the chair replace the hessian cover on the base to cover the webbing.

Stockists and Suppliers

John Lewis & Co., Ltd., Oxford Street, London, W.1. 'Jonelle' furnishing fabrics; hessian; calico; wadding; webbing; tacks; braid; buttons, etc.

Dunlop Ltd., manufacturers of latex and polyether foams.

Copydex, Ltd., 1, Torquay Street, London, W.2., manufacturers of Copydex latex adhesive, and Copydex tack punch.

Lister & Co., Ltd., Bradford, manufacturers of Dralon and other fibre velvets.

Sanderson & Co., Ltd., 56, Berners Street, London, W.1. Makers of furnishing fabrics.

The Kapok Co., London, N.W.10. Pure kapok for stuffing.

Arrow Fastener Co., Ltd. Manufacturers of staple-tackers and staples.